A tribute to the beauty of vintage denim. Includes a historical overview of denim jeans & denim fabric; a review of the denim fabric and denim jean manufacturing process; an in-depth "how-to" section to help you in re-creating your own vintage inspired denim masterpieces; and rare photographs of vintage denim to serve both as inspiration and a roadmap in your quest to Design • Detail • Create.

Denim Design Lab
© 2005 Brian Robbins

Text © 2005 Brian Robbins
All photographs © 2005 Brian Robbins, except as noted.

Cover image courtesy of Levi Strauss & Co. Archives, San Francisco. Photo by Hangauer/Kissinger © 2005.

All rights reserved. No part of this book may be reproduced or utilized in any form or by any means, electronic or mechanical (including photocopying, film or video recording, Internet posting, audio recording or any other information storage and retrieval system) without the prior permission in writing from the copyright owner.

Published in the United States by Denim Design Lab, LLC
P.O. Box 5853, San Clemente, CA 92674
phone- 949-366-3307
fax- 949-366-3304
e mail - denimdesignlab@aol.com
web site - denimdesignlab.com

ISBN-13: 9780977301201 (hard bound)
ISBN-10: 0-9773012-0-6 (hard bound)
Library of Congress Control Number: 2005908760

Printed and bound in Hong Kong.

TABLE OF CONTENTS

1. Intro — 1
2. The History of Denim Jeans — 5
3. The History of Denim Fabric — 32
4. Anatomy of a Levi's 501® Jean — 40
5. Anatomy of a Lee Cowboy Pant — 46
6. Manufacturing of Denim Jeans — 51
7. Denim Manufacturing Process — 55
8. Inspiration — 63
9. The Denim Design Lab™ — 81
10. Tools of the Trade — 83
11. Getting Started — 85
12. Finishing Details — 87
13. Glossary — 130

DENIM DESIGN LAB™

DESIGN·DETAIL·CREATE

INTRO

The beauty is in the details.

It is the subtlest of details that attract true denim aficionados to one pair over another. The ultimate display of detail is found in true vintage denim. Study (if you are lucky enough to get your hands on one) a pair of original Levi's 501XX jeans or other vintage styles that have been worn for years. The story of each wearer has been indelibly recorded on each pair.

Particular abrasion patterns, locations of wear and whiskering are tell tale signs of what each pair has lived through. Varying amounts of creasing and whiskering, and their location, are indicative of wearers who sat or crouched frequently. Clean, dark indigo, with little evidence of wear could be indicative of wearers who worked on their feet all day, likely indoors. Stains are further evidence of the type of life the wearer led. Grease and oil stains from the mechanic, paint drips and chalk smears from the painter, bleach stains from the laundry worker...

The book "Denim Design Lab™" is a tribute to the beauty of denim. The ageless fabric used to produce blue jeans, which, like fine wine, continues to get better with age. The "Denim Design Lab™" kit provides both a roadmap and the basic tools necessary to recreate many of the most common wear and stain details found in authentic vintage denim, as well as some of the most expensive vintage inspired styles currently being sold at retail.

Make no mistake about it, the process of recreating these looks is neither easy nor quick. The majority of work that goes into aging denim is done by hand. Some recreations of vintage originals can take up to five days of work to produce. However, for those who appreciate the level of detail and originality that can be achieved by following the right techniques and putting in the time, your efforts will be rewarded with truly original, one of a kind denim styles.

INTRO

Before embarking on your first creative endeavor, take the time to learn and appreciate denim's rich history and the detailed processes involved in bringing a pair of denim jeans to life.

In the pages that follow, you will learn about the history of both denim jeans and denim fabric, take a look under the hood of two of the most famous jeans in history, and learn about the process involved in making denim fabric and finished denim jeans a reality.

Once you have a firm grasp of denim's past and present, you can then start to contribute to its future. The roadmap outlined in these pages may be just the spark you need to start you on your way in creating your single most treasured denim masterpiece, or even the next big trend in denim.

Design • Detail • Create
Denim Design Lab™

The History of Denim Jeans

From the very first pair of waist overalls built by Levi Strauss & Co. to the multitude of denim labels available today, what is most amazing is that in over 130 years, how little has actually changed. This fact attests to the utility and design appeal of what is at the same time a piece of equipment and an indispensable article of casual clothing. Blue jeans are as much at home in mines and auto garages as in restaurants and on the cat walk. They are timeless and existed as naturally in the 1800's as they do today. Blue jeans are both common yet extremely unique and personal.

Miners, "Blue Eyes Mine" in California, 1882

THE HISTORY OF DENIM JEANS

The origin of the word "jeans" is ambiguous. Some believe the term came from a reference to the type of pants worn by sailors from Genoa, Italy; "Genoese" or "Genes." However, pants made of jean (not denim) were used as work-wear well before pants made of denim became the preferred fabric for work-wear. As denim pants became the overwhelming choice for work-wear, it appears the name jean became solely associated with this particular style of pant. Eloesser-Heynemann, the manufacturer of "Can't Bust 'Em's," were supposedly calling their black waist overalls "Frisko Jeens" as early as 1925.

Handbill advertising various LS&CO. products, c1899

Originally known as "Waist Overalls," the birth of blue jeans as we know them today (jeans or simply "denim" as they are now referred to) can be traced to 1873. The original jeans arose out of necessity, and filled a need for stronger, more durable and more comfortable work-wear for the gold miners and day laborers who wore them. Jeans were counted on as a piece of equipment, as important as the other tools in a workman's toolbox.

The History of Denim Jeans

Brands such as "Can't Bust 'Em" were selling what were referred to as jeans as early as the 1860's, approximately ten years prior to the time Levi Strauss & Co. introduced their soon-to-be -famous version. While jeans made out of denim were already being sold by this time, it was the collaboration between Levi Strauss and a tailor named Jacob Davis from Reno, Nevada (by way of Latvia) that marked the beginning of what would soon become the single most popular item of clothing in history.

Levi Strauss, c1800

Jacob Davis, date unknown

On 20 May, 1873, Levi Strauss and Jacob Davis were granted U.S. Patent #139,121 for an "Improvement in Fastening Pocket Openings." The application of copper rivets on to the stress points of men's work pants added incredible strength to the areas most susceptible to ripping. This simple improvement in design was enough to create a revolution in wearing apparel.

THE HISTORY OF
DENIM JEANS

The late 1800's and early 1900's saw the start up of numerous denim labels, each vying for a share of their local work-wear market. While only a few of these originators are still competing in today's denim market, some of the earliest blue jeans were produced by:

- Eloesser-Henemann (1851), "Can't Bust 'Em"
- Levi Strauss & Co. (1873), Levi's
- Hamilton Carhartt (1884), Carhartt
- OshKosh B'Gosh (1895), OshKosh
- Neustadter Brothers (pre-1900), Boss of the Road
- Hudson Overall Co. (1904), Hudson (later renamed the "Blue Bell Overall Co." in 1919)
- H.D. Lee Mercantile Company (1911), Lee
- Brownstein, Newmark & Louis (early 1900's), Stronghold
- Blue Bell (1919), Wrangler

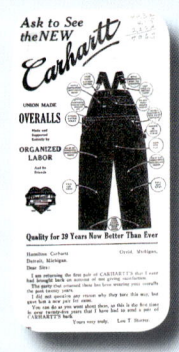

Many "co-branded" denim garments were also being sold during this time. For many consumers, just knowing the denim fabric came from Amoskeag, Erwin or Cone Mills, and was the appropriate weight (regardless of the manufacturere of the jeans), was enough to close the deal. Probably the best example of co-branding can be seen in the vintage garments found by James Harlan in an abandoned two-room shack near Greensboro, North Carolina. Some of these garments, in addition to an obscure local label, were clearly co-branded with the Cone "Deeptone Denim" label.

The History of Denim Jeans

When Levi Strauss & Co.'s patent for riveted pockets expired in 1890, the method of construction they started became the standard for nearly every subsequent pair of jeans made to date by all manufacturers.

Trade card, c1899

A staple work-wear uniform of early laborers, the first one-piece denim over-all was introduced by the H.D. Lee Mercantile Co. in 1913 and sold under the name "Union-Alls." The design proved so popular that in 1917 they became the official doughboy fatigue for the US Army during World War I.

THE HISTORY OF
DENIM JEANS

The iconic 12 1/2" tall "Buddy Lee" doll, complete with miniaturized authentic denim outfits, was created by Lee's first Union-All salesman Chester Reynolds in 1920 as a promotional item. The original Buddy Lee dolls remained in production for 40 years, until being retired in 1960. While originally available for a mere $1.00 in 1929, today perfect "BLD's" with original uniforms can fetch as much as $800.00 for collectors lucky enough to find one.

THE HISTORY OF DENIM JEANS

In 1927, Lee introduced a zip-up version of its Union-Alls. To help promote this first in work-wear, Lee held a naming contest for the garment; the winning name being the "Whizit," due to the sound made when zipped up and down. Babe Ruth was the first of many celebrity endorsers for this significant development in construction method.

"Lee's Rascal's" showing off their new "Whizit's"

THE HISTORY OF DENIM JEANS

The U.S. Stock Market crash of 1929 and the "Great Depression" that followed was a major contributing factor to the growth of denim during this time. The poor economy resulted in America's manual laborers being forced to live in their uniforms, which were, more often than not, made out of denim. Photos from this period in history will almost always show people clothed in denim work-wear - worn, stained, shredded and repaired. Their lives and struggles were visible to the outside world via the state of the clothing on their backs.

Denim became the standard issue material for uniforms of both Union workers and prisons. The increased demand for tough wearing work-wear led to an increase in denim manufacturers. While the market share of Levi Strauss & Co. and Lee were never really challenged, newer denim brands such as Big Bridge, Big Ben, Big Smith, Blue Bell, Buckhide, Carhartt, Oshkosh B'Gosh, Pay Day, Tuff Nut and Union Made were all attempting to supply the demand for denim. The merger of the Big Ben Manufacturing Company with the Blue Bell Overall Company in 1926 led to the formation of Wrangler, one of the strongest denim brands in America catering to mainly the Western market.

THE HISTORY OF DENIM JEANS

Photo of cowboys in Texas, c1902

Western movies and the growing popularity of Cowboys in the Western United States in the 1930's exposed a larger audience to blue jeans. Blue jeans became symbols of independence and individualism. Non-laborers wanting to emulate their Western heroes from the big screen sought out jeans in ever increasing numbers. "Dude Ranches," basically, functioning ranches catering to people who wanted to have

In-store advertising piece, 1950's

THE HISTORY OF DENIM JEANS

a taste of the Western lifestyle without much of the real work that takes place on a ranch, were hugely popular with Easterners.

To help market its jeans in the 1930's, Lee began to produce giant, twelve-foot-tall versions with "Lee Cowboy Pants" embroidered in bright orange thread across the seat. While initially hung at the site of rodeos, they were soon also being hung on telephone poles, the side of barns and in front of stores. An overall version of the oversized denim billboards was included in the Smithsonian Institute's "Signs of Life; Symbols in the City" display in 1976. Lee was a major contributor to not only the growth of the western wear category, but also in the establishment of both the "Rodeo Cowboy's Association" and the "Rodeo Information Commission" in the 30's.

Other important contributing factors in spreading the popularity of jeans at this time were the decline in price for early motorcars and the abundance of railroad tracks across America. This increased mobility helped expose jeans to more consumers and ensured that a steadier supply was available.

THE HISTORY OF DENIM JEANS

American Servicemen overseas during World War II in the 1940's helped introduce blue jeans to consumers outside of the U.S.A., and were often accosted by people wanting to buy the jeans they were wearing right on the spot. Global demand for jeans stemmed in large part from the exposure of these G.I.s stationed from Europe to Asia, as they were often wearing what was the first pair the locals had ever seen in person. These G.I.s were wearing what the Western stars were wearing in the movies they saw, and they had to get their hands on a pair.

Because of essential materials rationing during the war, LS&CO.'s blue jeans from this period lost the cinch back closure on the back of the waist, as well as the rivets located on the watch pocket and at the crotch. On top of reducing the overall number of rivets, to further save on copper, steel rivets with a copper finish were used for all remaining rivets. The double row of stitching on the back pockets, or Arcuate, was painted on to save thread. A large amount of the denim used to manufacture jeans for use by the U.S. Military during the war came from Cone Mills.

THE HISTORY OF DENIM JEANS

Because of the increasing demand for "Lee Rider" jeans, in 1944 Lee purchased the San Francisco based Eloesser-Heynemann Company. Best known for their black "Frisko Jeens" popular with miners, teamsters and firemen of the day, Eloesser-Heynemann's other brands included "Can't Bust 'Em," "Boss-of-the-Road," and "Copper King." The trademark "Can't Bust 'Em" would eventually resurface in 1998 as a slogan associated with Lee's "Lee Dungarees" label.

In post-war America, blue jeans became accepted as clothing for leisure, and not strictly for laborers and cowboys.

In-store advertising piece, 1950s

THE HISTORY OF
DENIM JEANS

Denim, still the uniform of non-conformity, was adopted as standard issue for "biker clubs." Many servicemen who road motorcycles during the war continued to ride upon their return home to the States. Some displayed aggressive riding habits and what was considered anti-social behavior. The rowdy events surrounding the 1947 AMA (American Motorcycle Association) "Gypsy Tour" in Hollister, CA were captured by the national media and painted a picture in the minds of many citizens that bikers were "denim-clad outlaws."

As they say, "There is no such thing as bad press." In the 1950's, blue jeans got their share of attention thanks to movies such as "The Wild One" (1954) with Marlon Brando (based on the 1947 Hollister event) and "Rebel Without a Cause" (1955) with James Dean.

THE HISTORY OF DENIM JEANS

Blue jeans began to be closely associated with "rebel bikers," juvenile delinquency and social outcasts.

To make matters worse (or better, as it created even more demand), Elvis Presley's sexually-drenched performance while wearing a denim jailhouse outfit in the 1957 film "Jailhouse Rock" did little to make conservative America supportive of denim as acceptable clothing for its kids. Many schools banned the wearing of blue jeans in school, which was basically a mandate to every kid that wanted to be "cool" to get their hands on a pair.

THE HISTORY OF DENIM JEANS

The 1950's saw wider distribution of blue jeans throughout the U.S.A. to a more diverse consumer base. With the expanding distribution came one of the few major changes to the original button fly waist overall; because of consumer demand and the growing popularity for zippers, LS&CO. added a zipper fly version to their offering for the first time in 1954. While dark shrink-to-fit 501 jeans (usually rolled at the cuffs) and a white t-shirt were the uniform of choice for the majority of youth in the 1950's, catering to the western wear market, Lee introduced "Lee Westerners" (also known as "Lee Whites") in 1959. Lee Westerners were the first white dress-up jeans, made from Lee's "Westweave" fabric and cut in slim western silhouettes.

THE HISTORY OF DENIM JEANS

Built as a promotional tool for the State Fair of Texas, Lee produced the largest pair of Lee Riders ever manufactured (at a massive 52 feet tall) in 1952. The jean (along with a shirt) built to clothe "Big Tex" took 364 hours to produce, consumed 100 yards of denim and 5,900 yards of thread.

THE HISTORY OF DENIM JEANS

By 1960, LS&CO. officially adopted the name "jeans" for what were previously referred to as "waist overalls" or, after about 1900, just "overalls." This change in name was the result of the company aligning their product with what the majority of young consumers were already calling these pants.

Many of these new consumers were American college students who commonly participated in anti-war protests. Images of American youth who rallied against the establishment were common in newspapers, magazines and on TV programs during this time; more often than not, they were wearing denim. As with their counterparts from the 1950's, denim was again associated with rebels and individuality, and blue jeans were their uniform of choice.

Peace loving hippies during this "Woodstock" era were among the first to customize their denim; cutting and fraying the hems, applying patches and decorative fabrics and writing anti-war slogans on their jeans. As with the musicians they worshiped, it was difficult to find anyone during this period "not" wearing denim jeans.

The popularity of jeans in the 1960's among women led to denim jeans becoming one of the only true unisex garments (the other being the basic T-Shirt). Unlike in the 1950's when most wore their denim tight and tapered, and the preference was for dark and crisp looking jeans, in the mid to late 1960's clothes, and denim

THE HISTORY OF DENIM JEANS

in particular, was worn loose. "Bell-bottom" leg flares were in... some say this trend had something to do with the speed at which you could take your pants off... after denim, "nothing" was the uniform of choice for many flower children of the day.

As the generation of Rock n' Roll, protests, Woodstock and free love came to an end, Disco was there to help usher in the 1970's. Huge collared lapels to go along with huge bell-bottoms and synthetic fiber leisure suits put up a serious threat to the tried and true 501 jean.

Spring 1972 price list for jeans

As a sign of the times, in 1972 Lee produced its very own take on this challenge to fashion with the introduction of the "Leesure Suit;" A one piece garment based on a standard 5-pocket jean with matching jacket attached. It was marketed as a "sportier alternative to traditional office attire."

The History of Denim Jeans

Denim had grown from the uniform of the counter culture to an outright status symbol in the 1970's. Like no other time before this, what you wore was seen to define who you were. While leisure suits clad the mainstream looking to be cool, and designer denim clad the rich and those desperately wanting to look like they were, traditional denim jeans still found their way onto the most influential artists, actors, writers and rock stars; the cultural elite of the decade.

Denim made its first appearance on the cover of Vogue in January 1971 and was the controversial focal point on the cover of the Rolling Stones album "Sticky Fingers." For those who could possibly have missed it... it featured a provocative photograph by Andy Warhol of the crotch area of a guy wearing jeans, and featured a real functioning zipper.

Denim's upscale acceptance can be summed up by a quote from the popular fashion designer of the time, Bill Blass, with his statement that "Levi's are the best single item of apparel ever designed." Denim was becoming big business and upscale brands such as Gloria Vanderbilt and Calvin Klein were among the first to leverage this success by launching high priced jeans collections geared towards fashion conscious consumers. Vanderbilt sold jeans in a multitude of colors with her trademark "swan" logo on the back pockets. She was also one of the first to use stretch denim. These innovations, along with her well-known family name, helped launch one of the original "designer labels." Calvin Klein, on the other hand, exploded onto the designer denim scene through his sex driven marketing campaign. The 15-year-old Brooke Shields' statement that "Nothing comes between me and my Calvin's" was the cause of both enormous controversy and enormous sales.

THE HISTORY OF
DENIM JEANS

Alongside the exploding designer market being created for denim, blue jeans continued to be used as a blank canvas for new forms of expression during the 1970's. Decorating one's denim was a popular outlet for personal expression, by both high-end designer labels as well as at the consumer level. Paint, embroidery, beads, sequins and patches were all applied to jeans in various degrees to create unique wearable art.

Many of the original techniques used by consumers to make their jeans more original, from the days of Woodstock through the 1970's, are still used in the production of today's denim styles.

The History of Denim Jeans

In 1974, Lee began to market "pre-washed" jeans in response to consumer demand for jeans with a softer hand. Lee's foray into the finishing side of denim manufacturing began after one of its manufacturing supervisors sent a just built raw pair to a local laundry to try to soften it up. The "wet process" they started experimenting with in 1973 turned into a multi-million dollar finishing venture by 1982, as stonewashed jeans became part of Lee's core denim line.

Based largely on the commercial success of Vanderbilt and Klein, designer denim continued as a huge category in the 1980's. Capitalizing on the enduring success and universal appeal of denim at the time, designers seized the opportunity to bring denim to new heights; at least in regards to the prices consumers were willing to pay. The emphasis was initially on fit and the name of the designer emblazoned on the label. As more and more competitors entered the fray (Jordache, Guess?, Sassoon, Sergio Valente, etc.), the need to differentiate their product from each other drove product innovation. The focus turned to different finishing techniques, and both stone and acid washing became commonplace. Manufacturers experimented with golf balls, old shoes, rocks, tires and whatever else they could get their hands on to wash with their jeans to create worn, vintage and/or unique finishes. The material they found that worked the best, and which is still in use today, is pumice stone (a light-weight volcanic rock). Other popular trends being commercialized at this time were ripped, torn, frayed and repaired detailing. To balance out the heavily worn denim offerings in its collections, Lee introduced its "Dress Blues," jeans finished with indigo dyes designed to retain their dark blue color. Old was new and worn-out was hip. Denim again proved to be a chameleon, as perfect a fit in a garage, on a campus, or in a club, and worn as often by punk rockers, presidents and fashion models.

THE HISTORY OF DENIM JEANS

By 1985 the red thread line, or "selvage," that was present on the inside of both legs began to disappear from 501 jeans. This occurred as a result of changes to manufacturing equipment as the original 30" shuttle looms were slowly replaced by much larger 60"+ looms beginning in 1983. While seemingly insignificant, this single change became a signpost for collectors that would identify styles made up to this date as more valuable and collectible.

Lee began selling its "Storm Rider" line in 1986, which featured holes and rips in each pair. The ads for these jeans carried the tag line "Only jeans that fit this well, get the chance to look this bad." In 1987, Lee introduced some of the first "acid washed" (chemically stonewashed) jeans in the market under the "Frosted Riders" name.

The biggest change to jeans in the 1990's was in the silhouette; the size, or more precisely, their "oversize." Hip-Hop ruled the decade for much of America's youth, and the bigger your jeans were, the cooler you were. Belts were optional, and purposely left behind in the urban community as a sign of incarceration (belts were taken away from prisoners upon entering prison). The cuts were ultra baggy

THE HISTORY OF DENIM JEANS

and worn perilously close to falling off. The trends were driven by urban music producers and performers such as Russell Simmons, the founder of Def Jam Records (Phat Pharm, 1996) and Sean "P. Diddy" Combs (Sean John, 2001).

On the designer denim front, high fashion designers such as Helmut Lang were finishing their denim with paint drip stains and tints to create what is now referred to as "dirty denim," and in the process commanding more than 10 times the price of basic branded denim.

Today's denim market is filled with hundreds of competitors globally. While the originals are still around and account for the majority of market share in the U.S.A. (LS&CO., Lee & Wrangler), newer innovators such as Diesel, G-Star and Guess? have staked their claim to the future of the denim market. European and Japanese denim brands have contributed amazing fabrication, fit and finishing details to the market.

While the overall silhouette of today's denim remains immediately recognizable, the level of detail that goes into building many of today's styles has definitely increased from the 1800's.

THE HISTORY OF
DENIM JEANS

Drawing from long histories and extensive design archives, both LS&CO. (Levi's® Vintage Clothing) and Lee (Lee Authentics) have launched very successful sub-brands that strive to recreate the vintage masterpieces currently stored in their vaults. By authentically reproducing the original garments, in fit, fabric, construction, finish, trim and labeling, they allow modern denim enthusiasts to wear jeans from denim's glorious past. The following garments are some of the best examples of authentic vintage recreations.

Limited Edition 501® XX Jean

From Levi's® Vintage Clothing. A recreation of an 1886 501® XX Jean.

THE HISTORY OF DENIM JEANS

Limited Edition "Indigo Immortal" 501® Jean

From Levi's® Vintage Clothing. A recreation of the first 5 pocket 501® Jean, c1901.

THE HISTORY OF DENIM JEANS

Lee 101B Men's Jean

From Lee Authentics. A recreation inspired by their 101 Cowboy pants, c1940

Photos courtesy of Lee Jeans.

The History of Denim Jeans

Lee 101B Women's Jean

From Lee Authentics. A recreation inspired by their 101 Cowboy pants, c1940

Photos courtesy of Lee Jeans.

THE HISTORY OF DENIM

So, where did the term "denim" come from?

Some claim the term denim was derived from the French term "serge de Nimes," meaning a serge fabric from the French mill town of Nimes. As serge is a twill fabric, this particular one made of wool blended with silk, it is unlikely that denim as we know it today had its origins here. In the 17th century in France, there was also a wool blend fabric being sold called "nim." Again, it is unlikely that today's denim had its origins from this fabric.

In England around the 1600's, there was a twill fabric being sold called "de nim," but it is likely that merchants gave this fabric a French sounding name hoping to make it sound imported and exotic. Also very popular at this time in England was a fabric known as "jean." Jean was a cotton, linen &/or wool blend that had its origins in Genoa, Italy. Although initially imported in large quantities from Italy, by the end of the 1600's, this blended fabric was being produced in Lancashire, England. At some point prior to the 18th century, the jean fabric produced in England began to be made exclusively out of cotton, and was noted as being very durable. A fundamental difference between jean and what became known as "denim," was that jean was woven using two like colored threads, while denim used two different ones, one white and one colored (soon to be almost exclusively indigo blue). While jean fabric was noted as sturdy, it was used primarily for suiting, whereas denim was almost exclusively reserved for work-wear. Due to England's existing fabric industry and its established trade relations with American companies, it is most likely that denim as we know it made its way to America via England, rather than France or Italy.

Denim in America

Cotton denim was produced by a number of American mills on a small scale as early as 1789. One of the earliest written mentions of the word denim was the technical sketches o

THE HISTORY OF DENIM

denim weaving methods included in the 1792 book called "The Weavers Draft Book and Clothiers Assistant." The manufacturing of fabric, including denim, was one of the original industries started in New England. As Americans sought both literal and economic independence from England, the local production of formerly imported goods such as denim were a high priority.

The invention of the cotton gin in 1793 helped ensure America's place as the number one supplier of cotton to the world during the early 19th Century. The income generated from the export of cotton was a major source of financing for America's rapidly developing industrial economy. The tremendous output of America's southern cotton plantations ensured a steady supply of the raw material needed to produce denim.

The first waist overalls manufactured in America were made from denim produced at the Amoskeag Manufacturing Company in Manchester, New Hampshire. This mill was founded in 1804 and was producing denim beginning in the mid-1800's. In the 1870's, Amoskeag was a major supplier of denim to Levi Strauss & Co. The oldest known surviving pair of Levi's waist overalls, produced in San Francisco circa 1879, was made from denim produced from the Amoskeag Mill. The Amoskeag Mill closed its doors in 1936.

THE HISTORY OF DENIM

By 1915, the majority of the denim used by Levi Strauss & Co. was produced by Cone Mills in North Carolina, and by 1922 Cone was the exclusive source of denim used for all Levi's® 501® jeans. Speaking of Cone, no real discussion on the history of denim fabric in America would be possible without mention of the Cone Export & Commission Co. (now known as "Cone Denim") and their impact on and contribution to the denim market.

Cone Denim, currently one of the largest manufacturers of denim in the world, actually got its start as a marketing company. Founded in 1891 in New York by the brothers Moses and Caesar Cone as the "Cone Export & Commission Co.," they were instrumental in bringing denim manufacturing to the American South and setting the standard for modern, efficient denim manufacturing.

Prior to the establishment of the Cone Export & Commission Co., denim manufacturing was a monopoly of mills located in the Northern States (such as Amoskeag). While the required raw material, cotton, was grown in the South, the finishing of fabrics (including denim) was thought to only be possible in the North. Within their first year of operation, the Cone brothers quickly organized approximately 90% of the 50 Southern mills. Under their representation, these mills diversified their operations and were soon producing all types of fabrics, previously thought impossible in the South. Basing manufacturing near the source of raw materials was a significant improvement in operating structure, and provided an immediate economic benefit.

The Cone brothers went from a selling & marketing agency to manufacturing outright in 1895 when they opened the Proximity Manufacturing Company in Greensboro, North Carolina.

THE HISTORY OF DENIM

The name "Proximity" was used to represent the closeness of the mill to the vast cotton fields, cotton gins, warehouses, highways and railroad lines near by. In 1896, the first cut of denim was woven at Proximity. Other than during a few years in the 1960's, from 1896 to the mill's closure in 1978, for 82 straight years Proximity produced nothing but denim fabric. At its peak in 1951, Proximity was producing 49 million yards of denim per year. Even with this incredible output, they could still not keep up with the demand for their denim. As a result of its current demand and foresight into the future of denim, Cone built what is still to this day one of the world's largest denim mills, "White Oak Mills," in Greensboro, North Carolina in 1905. Today, output at White Oak Mills is approximately 40 million yards per year.

Cone's influence on the denim market during this time can be surmised by a quote from a denim book written in 1925 by

THE HISTORY OF DENIM

Carl J. Balliett with the statement "The denim market came to look to Ceasar Cone to forecast the demand, to set the pace in production. The Cone cost in production and the Cone price stabilized the world market."

A Fortunate Accident...

Following an estimated 6 inches of rain in 24 hours that fell on downtown Greensboro on 15 June, 1969, Cone Mills was certain they had one hell of a mess to clean up after. On top of damage to machinery and forced cancellation of shifts due to the serious flooding, one of their main warehouses containing millions of yards of denim flooded. The denim was soaked and at risk of mildewing. While the fabric was being washed and dried by an army of local high school students trying to save it, a merchandiser from Cone's New York Marketing Division suggested that the White Oak mill run all the soaked denim through a solution to randomly remove the indigo dye and give the denim a faded, mottled appearance. The likely disaster became a profitable innovation with the unlikely creation of the first bleached production jean, aptly named "Pinto Wash Denim®." Response from designers, manufacturers, retailers and young consumers was immediate and the project a complete success.

Denim Variations & Innovations

Up until about 1897, all blue denim was dyed using natural indigo dye. Natural indigo is derived from the fermentation of leaves from the indigofera, storobilanthes or polygonum plants, however, the vast majority of early denim was dyed using indigo derived from the indigofera plant. A unique feature of indigo is that it does not bond strongly to the cotton fibers in denim. As such, repeated wear and washing causes the dye to lift from the surface of the fibers, while leaving the underlining fibers largely intact. The result is denim's million different faces, each pair completely unique

The History of Denim

from each other, and each pair constantly changing, from the first time you wear them to the last.

In 1880, a German chemist by the name of Johann Friedrich Wilhelm Adolf von Baeyer was the first person to synthesize indigo. The German company BASF was the first to develop a commercially viable manufacturing process for synthetic indigo, and due to its reduced costs and increased availability, by 1913, the use of natural indigo was almost completely nonexistent. In 1917, Cone Mills was the first manufacturer to use alternate dye stuffs (non indigo) on its denim, as well as the first to offer colors other than the traditional indigo blue.

THE HISTORY OF DENIM

H.D. Lee introduced overalls made of from what they called "Jelt Denim" (made from Cone's style 818) in 1925. The fabric, made from tightly twisted yarns, claimed to be the strongest and bluest 11.5oz denim available, and as hard wearing as traditional 13oz denim. Jelt Denim was advertised as "the best denim in America."

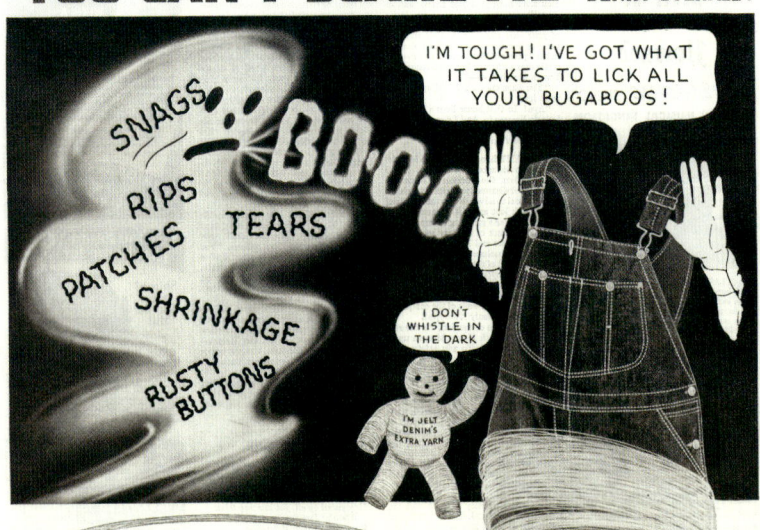

THE HISTORY OF DENIM

To drive this point home, in 1939 Lee's marketing campaign included a series of cartoon-like ads based on "Ripley's Believe It or Not!" focusing on the strength of the fabric.

In one ad, the tires of a racecar were covered with Jelt, and after racing for 50 miles, the fabric was stated to be "still whole and good." In another, the Jelt was said to have endured being run over 100 times by a 5-ton steamroller.

Other ads in the campaign claimed the Jelt maintained its color and fit, even after being washed, dried and ironed 200 times, and did not wear out after being subjected to the equivalent of a marathon walked on untreated concrete on the knees of one Tom Boyd. **Believe It, Or Not...?**

THE HISTORY OF DENIM

Wrangler claimed to be the first to offer black dyed denim in 1950. Originally used to produce an outfit for Hopalong Cassidy, a popular TV and rodeo personality of the time, black denim has continued to be a staple item in many denim lines sold today. Rather than being dyed with indigo, a black dye is used, and rather than fading to a light blue, black denim tends to fade to a frosty gray.

Another innovation, first used by Wrangler in 1964, was the broken twill weave. This style of denim was invented by John Neil Walker and different in that its diagonal twill lines changed direction. On top of the unique surface texture, this weave also prevented the legs from twisting, which was a common occurrence in jeans made on the old shuttle looms of the time.

One of the most significant changes in the production of denim fabric occurred as a result of efficiency. With the world's never ending appetite for denim only increasing during the late 1970's, manufacturers began to shift their weaving machinery from 27" – 30" shuttle looms to much larger 60"+ modern versions. The increased width added efficiency and lowered the price of finished denim, and in general produced a much more uniform and consistent finish. However, the slubs and other irregularities found in the vintage, pre-1985 denim was what many found so appealing. As significant as the change in surface texture, with the (temporary) demise of the original shuttle looms also came the demise of selvage.

THE HISTORY OF DENIM

The new 60" denim did not have the immediately recognizable selvage edge on either side of the fabric to keep it from unraveling. Soon after this change, jeans that could be found made with the distinctive vintage selvage fabric became instant collectors items. To this day, the appearance of selvage is probably the single most recognized sign that a pair of jeans is either vintage or an expensive replica.

In 1986, a patent was granted to the Italian based Candida Laundry Company for the process of "acid washing" denim. The first to actually commercialize this process on jeans was the Italian based company "Rifle." The effect was achieved by putting pumice stones soaked with chlorine into industrial washers with the jeans. The irregular bleached results of this wash were also called Marble Wash, Moon Wash and Snow Wash. Lee introduced its version, "Frosted Riders," in 1987.

In 1962, Cone Mills became the first American fabric mill to produce and market stretch denim. With technical advancements in the production of synthetic fibers, mills were able to add Lycra and other stretch materials to the cotton in their denim. While the surface look changed little if at all, the new blends enabled designers to experiment with slimmer fits and offer comfortable alternatives to traditional denim jeans.

ANATOMY OF A
LEVI'S 501® JEAN

Anatomy of a Levi's® 501® jean...
The very first 501® jeans were built in 1873, and were at the time referred to as "waist overalls." They had one back pocket with exposed rivets, the Arcuate stitching design, a small watch pocket, a back cinch, suspender buttons and a single rivet in the crotch area. These earliest versions were made with 9oz. ecru selvage XX blue denim.

The Arcuate, the double row of orange &/or yellow stitching on the back pockets of Levi Strauss & Co.'s denim jeans is one of the oldest surviving apparel trademarks. Up until 1947, the Arcuate design was applied by means of a single needle sewing machine. As this was a manual process done by hand, it was virtually impossible to ensure that the Arcuate design turned out exactly the same each time. This resulted in uneven and often crooked looking designs. From 1947 on, a double needle sewing machine helped ensure that each Arcuate design was even and consistent. On these post-war versions, a "diamond" shape at the bottom of the Arcuate is created where the two lines of stitching meet because of the use of the double-needle machines.

With the popularity of LS&CO.'s denim jeans increasing by the day, the need to clearly separate their product from the competition grew. Real leather patches were first used in 1873, but it was not until 1886 that the universally recognized leather patch depicting two horses pulling a pair of jeans in opposite directions was added to the back of each pair at the waistband.

ANATOMY OF A LEVI'S 501® JEAN

Beginning in the 1950's, LS&CO. went from a real leather patch to a heavy-duty card stock "leather-like" version to save cost.

The timeless model number "501®" originated as a lot or ordering number used by retailers to purchase LS&CO.'s particular model of denim jeans beginning in approximately 1890. Prior to this time, the model was known as "XX."

In approximately 1901, the 2nd back pocket was added and the pants began to be referred to as simply "overalls."

In 1922, belt loops were added to the waistbands, although both the suspender buttons and cinchback remained. Due to the redundancy of both a cinchback and a belt, you will often see originals from this period (as well as some vintage remakes) with the cinch straps cut off, leaving just two sewn squares on the back.

ANATOMY OF A
LEVI'S 501® JEAN

Between 1927 and 1930, Cone Mills started producing 10oz. red selvage denim exclusively for 501 jeans. The selvage is visible on the inside of the outer seam of each leg and in the inside seam of most small coin pockets. The distinctive red stitch line ("aka mimi") was added to the all white selvage to differentiate the denim for LS&CO. from other denim brands that purchased its fabric from Cone Mills.

With the adoption of more efficient and cost effective 60" wide looms in 1983, Cone Mills stopped general production of its red selvage denim and in its place, the wider XXX denim was used.

ANATOMY OF A LEVI'S 501® JEAN

Up until 1937, all 501 jeans used rivets on both the front and back pockets (as well as a single rivet at the crotch area). Beginning in 1937, because of complaints from both cowboys and teachers that the rivets on the back pockets scratched their saddles and school desk chairs respectively, the rivets were covered up.

Concealed copper rivets

ANATOMY OF A LEVI'S 501® JEAN

The single crotch rivet disappeared from 501 jeans in the 1940's, largely because of complaints regarding the "heat conducting" effect the copper rivet produced in this very sensitive area. During World War II, Levi Strauss & Co. did its part in the war effort by voluntarily removing a number of rivets in order to help conserve vital metal. Removed during this time were the two rivets that secured the cinch device, the two rivets that secured the small watch pocket and the single crotch rivet. In addition, the decorative Arcuate stitching design was removed, and in its place, the design was painted on to save thread. The back pocket rivets were removed for good in 1966 and replaced with reinforced stitching or "bar tacks."

From the beginning, all LS&CO.'s denim jeans had a total of four pockets; one back pocket, two front pockets and one small coin (or watch) pocket above the front right pocket. It was not until 1901 that the 5th pocket was added (the 2nd back pocket) to 501 jeans. Belt loops were added in 1922 and initially shared the waistband with suspender buttons, but by 1937 the suspender buttons were removed altogether.

Side by side with the Arcuate stitching, LS&CO. added another identifier to the right back pocket of 501 jeans in 1936, the red fabric "LEVI'S" Tab (or "Tab device"). Up until the 1950's the white lettering, in all capital letters, was woven onto only one side of the Tab. Some of these early red Tabs can be found without any writing on them at all (this allowed LS&CO. to register the red Tab alone as a trademark). From 1971, Levi's was written in lower case on all Tab devices ("Levi's") with the exception of the initial capital "L."

ANATOMY OF A LEVI'S 501® JEAN

A zippered version was added in 1954 and sold under the name "501® Z Jeans." Pre-shrunk versions were released in approximately 1961, and still sold under the "501® Jeans" name. The standard 5-pocket jean has remained almost completely unchanged to this day.

2003 marked both the 150th anniversary of the founding of LS&CO., as well as the 130th birthday of the 501 jean. To help mark the occasion, a limited edition re-make of a 1917 501 jean was produced under the Levi's® Vintage Clothing line. Only 501 units of these jeans were produced, and each pair sold for $501.00 each. To this day, these replicas still show up on EBay, offered at prices that make the original $501.00 seem affordable. An original vintage pair of these jeans is featured on pgs. 74 & 75.

ANATOMY OF A
LEE 101 COWBOY PANT

Anatomy of a Lee 101 Cowboy Pant...
Lee's 101 Cowboy Pants were first introduced in 1924 and were designed for the needs of America's cowboys and rodeo riders. Early ads stated they were "the only cowboy pants to incorporate Sanforized® 11.5 oz cowboy denim, U-shaped saddle crotch, scratch-proof hip pocket rivets, and a hot-iron branded hair-on-hide label."

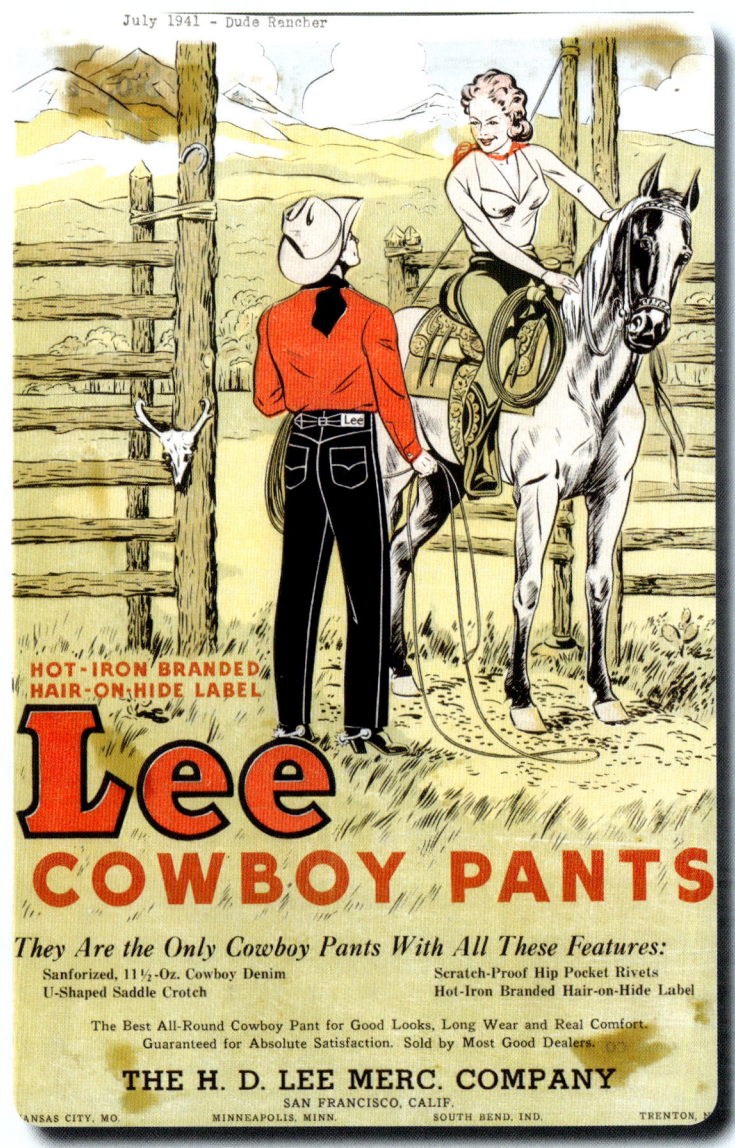

ANATOMY OF A
LEE 101 COWBOY PANT

H.D. Lee

The 101 jeans used a signature orange thread in their production. While they initially featured an arcuate stitching pattern extremely similar to that of LS&CO.'s 501 jeans, they eventually switched, in 1944, to the "Lazy S" curve (also known as the "compound curve"). This pocket pattern remains on many Lee jeans to this day. The "S" curve is said to represent the horns of a longhorn steer or the shape of the back of an occupied saddle.

In 1924, the back pocket rivets were removed because of complaints from cowboys that the metal rivets scratched their leather saddles. In their place, Lee applied its now widely recognizable signature "X" bar-tack stitching. Although originally only available as a button fly, in 1926, the "Amazing Hookless Fastener" (zipper) was introduced for the first time on Lee's 101 jeans. Lee's unique "U-Shaped Saddle Crotch" was also introduced in 1926. This change in the design pattern ensured a tailored fit by basing the rise and seat proportions off of the particular waist and inseam measurements, resulting in a more comfortable fit for cowboys. Upon receiving a trademark for the term "Riders" in 1935, Lee began to market its 101 Cowboy Pants under the name "Lee Riders."

ANATOMY OF A
LEE 101 COWBOY PANT

Beginning with its Buckle Back Riders in 1936, soon all Lee 101 Cowboy Pants featured a "hair-on-hide" label above the back right pocket. This was a leather patch, with the hair still attached, branded with the "Lee" trademark.

In 1944, the hair-on-hide label was replaced by the hairless, smooth leather "Twitch label," still in use on today's models. The wavy Lee logo branded on each Twitch label is meant to symbolize the twitching of a steer when being branded. While each patch was branded by hand until 1946, today's leather patch machinery can cut and brand approximately 50,000 patches each day.

The fit of Lee 101 Cowboy Pants became slimmer in 1941 at the request of cowboys and rodeo riders such as Turk Greenough. As the story goes, during a gathering of cowboys and Lee executives, Turk's wife Sally Rand (an exotic fan dancer) ripped out the seams of a pair of jeans and re-pinned them on her husband with a new tighter fit. The new tight-fitting "Lee Riders" (a name coined by Chester

ANATOMY OF A
LEE 101 COWBOY PANT

Reynolds in 1935) quickly became Lee's most popular style and were considered the "best fitting cowboy pants on the market" during this time.

Although Lee's 101 Cowboy Pants received minor updates in keeping pace with the changing fashion trends of the 1950's, they always maintained the core qualities and original design features that created such demand for them in the 1940's.

ANATOMY OF A
LEE 101 COWBOY PANTS

April 1941 - Dude Rancher

HOT-IRON BRANDED
HAIR-ON-HIDE LABEL

Lee
COWBOY PANTS

THE ONLY COWBOY PANT WITH ALL THESE FEATURES: Sanforized 11½-ounce Cowboy Denim; V-Shaped Saddle Crotch; Scratch-Proof Hip Pocket Rivets; Hot-Iron Branded Hair-on-Hide Label; Good Fit; Good Looks. Guaranteed. Sold by most good dealers.

THE H. D. LEE MERC. COMPANY

KANSAS CITY, MO.   SAN FRANCISCO, CALIF.   MINNEAPOLIS, MINN.

BY FAR THE BEST BUY IN A COWBOY PANT

MANUFACTURING
DENIM JEANS

The advancements in production equipment and processes have significantly decreased the amount of time it takes to produce a pair of raw denim jeans today. By far the most time consuming part is the laundering and finishing.

To build one pair of raw 5-pocket jeans takes on average 9 1/2 minutes, and can involve as many as 30 people. As mentioned in the beginning of this book, some detailed vintage replicas can take as long as 5 days of finishing to achieve an authentic look.

Below is a brief overview of the major steps involved, using modern manufacturing methods and equipment, to produce a pair of denim jeans.

Cutting:
An automatic spreader is used to lay down as much as 500 yards of denim fabric on a cutting table, in approximately 68 layers, at one time. An automatic cutting machine is programmed with the particular pattern to cut. Enough pieces are cut for approximately 34 pairs of jeans at the same time.

MANUFACTURING
DENIM JEANS

Preliminary Details:
Before the main sections are sewn together, all the smaller pattern pieces are assembled as necessary. This includes the zippers (if used), pockets, watch pocket, pocket detailing and belt loops.

Sewing Assembly:
The pattern pieces travel through approximately 15 different steps along the sewing line. Most of these processes are completed using manual sewing machines. The two main front and two main back panels are assembled separately until they are joined by the outside seam, waist band and inseam, respectively. After the belt loops, rivets and buttons have been attached, the final processes are creating the button hole(s) and sewing up the bottom hems.

MANUFACTURING
DENIM JEANS

Laundry:
There are five basic "wet processes" used, depending on the final look desired.

1. **Rinse** The most basic process takes a raw garment and simply removes the starch and sizing. A softener may also be applied to the jean at this point.

2. **Bleach** Actual bleach is used to lighten up the color of the denim.

3. **Stonewash** Used to create a worn, faded look, stonewashing can be achieved by adding either pumice stones or an enzyme such as Perlite into an industrial sized washer with the jeans.

4. **Chemical Wash** This process also includes the use of pumice stones, however

MANUFACTURING
DENIM JEANS

the pumice is first soaked in potassium permanganate. The addition of this liquid causes a blotchy "acid wash" look.

5. **Blast** This is the most recently developed and expensive manual process used in traditional laundering. Fine sand is "blasted" through a hose at high speeds and targeted to specific areas of the denim to cause large areas of fade and wear. A round of stonewashing sometimes also follows the blasting process.

Finishing:
Finishing encompasses all of the additional detail work used to create unique features on the jean, including staining, abrasion, wear marks, holes, repairs, patches, embroidery and other embellishments.

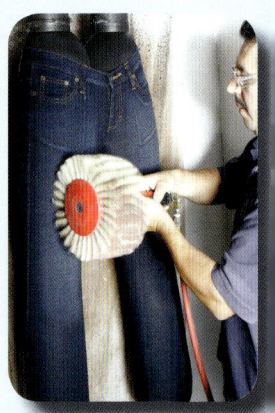

Following the particular finishing regiment, the jean is then steamed, inspected and labeled, in preparation for shipping to retail.

THE DENIM MANUFACTURING PROCESS

It is safe to say that most consumers never give much thought to the process of making denim fabric. It is assumed, as with most commodities, that it could not be that tough to manufacture... just a lot of cotton threads dyed blue and woven together, right? While the finishing of denim jeans usually gets all the attention and glory, the truth is that without high-quality denim as the blank canvas upon which to finish, high-end denim jeans would just not look and feel the way they do.

In reality, the manufacturing of denim fabric is an extremely technical and time-consuming process. The more you get to know about the process, the more you will appreciate the denim you are wearing. Overall, the process can be divided into two halves; the manufacturing of the yarns and the manufacturing of the fabric. Below is a brief overview of the major steps involved using modern manufacturing methods and equipment.

Yarn Manufacturing:

There are two main types of yarns used to produce denim, ring spun and open-end. Yarns produced using the ring spinning method are generally stronger and softer than those produced using the open-end method. Ring spun yarns result in denim with unique surface characteristics, including unevenness and slubs, which give jeans an irregular authentic vintage look. As the open-end method results in fibers that do not all end up parallel to the axis of the yarn, they are usually not as strong or soft as an equally sized ring spun yarn.

THE DENIM MANUFACTURING PROCESS

1. **Opening & Cleaning** (Ring Spun & Open-End Spun Yarns)

After an initial cleaning with a cotton gin, where the seeds are removed from the raw cotton, the cotton is formed into compressed bales. The bales (approximately 500 lbs. each) are then opened to let the cotton expand and allow further cleaning to take place. Leaf particles, dust and other foreign elements are removed with the help of a cleaning machine, which also fluffs and blends the cotton to help achieve a uniform fiber cross-section in preparation for the next step.

2. **Carding** (Ring Spun & Open-End Spun Yarns)

During this stage, further cleaning takes place as the cotton is aligned, and short fibers removed. A thin cotton web or mat is formed and fed into the card (machine) which converts the web into a condensed, fragile rope called a "sliver." If the sliver will be used for Open-End spinning, it is ready to be spun into yarn. If it will be used for Ring Spun yarn, it must continue on to "drawing."

3. **Drawing** (Ring Spun Yarns)

The drawing process is used to blend slivers together for better weight uniformity and fiber characteristics. During this stage, the fibers are further straightened in preparation for the next process. To produce one strand of drawing sliver, six strands of card silver must be combined in a process called "drafting."

THE DENIM MANUFACTURING PROCESS

4. **Roving** (Ring Spun Yarns)

The slivers are drafted into a smaller and finer form during the roving process. Each inch of drawing sliver produces four inches of roving. While the cotton roving resembles a thick yarn at this point, it is actually only strong enough to make it through the spinning process.

5. **Ring Spinning** (Ring Spun Yarns)

The roving is further drafted and twisted to the point that it finally starts to look like a thread. The yarns are formed into the desired size as they are passed through drafting rolls and aprons. One pound of denim yarn can be as long as 3 to 5 miles if laid end to end. During the ring spinning process, specialized attachments on the spinning frame can be used to create slubs and other imperfections to mimic the look of vintage denim.

6. **Winding** (Ring Spun Yarns)

The final stage for ring spun yarns before they are woven into fabric is winding. During this stage, unwanted yarn defects are cut out and then the yarn is spliced back together by a twin disc. The use of a twin disc creates an almost undetectable splice in a repaired yarn, which used to require the tying of a knot to repair. The smaller bobbins from the ring spinning stage are wound into larger "packages," now ready for use as either warp or weft in the weaving stage.

THE DENIM MANUFACTURING PROCESS

7. **Open-End Spinning** (Open-End Spun Yarns)

Unlike in the ring spinning process, the open end spinning process combines four steps into one (drawing, roving, spinning & winding). The carded sliver passes through a combing roll, which parallels the fibers. It is then fed through a rotor that uses both air and rotation to spin the yarn. The open-end yarn that comes out of the rotor is wound onto the same type of package as ring spun yarns, which use the winding process. Open-end spinning is said to be one of the most efficient methods of producing yarn. Yarn known as Amsler Open-End, or "Faux Ring Spun," is made using technology that creates slub patterns and other imperfections on open-end yarns that resemble more vintage looking ring spun yarns.

Fabric Manufacturing:

1. **Warping**

Up to 450 packages of yarn are threaded through a rack unit called a "creel." This process separates and parallels the individual yarns as they pass through a comb. During this process, with tension on both ends of the yarn, it is condensed as it passes through a trumpet and then wound into what is called a "ball warp" or "rope." The ropes are then ready for the indigo dyeing process.

THE DENIM
MANUFACTURING PROCESS

Warpers in Cone Denim's White Oak Plant, 1909. Photograph provided by Cone Denim.

THE DENIM MANUFACTURING PROCESS

2. Dyeing

The process of dyeing with indigo is unique in that the indigo only adheres to the outer ring of the thread, and does not soak through to the core of the fibers. Denim is a yarn dyed fabric, meaning its yarns are dyed before weaving (as opposed to a garment dye). The process of dyeing denim is called rope or long chain dyeing. The ropes from each of the ball warps pass through a series of boxes containing indigo dye. In between each dip, the ropes go through a process called "skying," where they are exposed to the air to allow the dye to oxidize and set. While the ropes are initially a bright green, with continued exposure to air and additional coats of indigo, they begin to turn blue. After several dips, the yarn is passed over steam-heated cans to dry and then coiled into large holding tubs to await the next process.

3. Beaming

In the beaming process, the dyed ropes are separated and paralleled through a comb into individual strands of yarn. The yarns are then wound onto a "section beam" in preparation for the next step.

4. Slashing

The purpose of this process is to give the dyed warp yarns the flexibility and strength to survive the stress of the weaving process. A protective coating called "warp size" (a heavy starch solution) is applied by dipping the yarns in the "sizing" solution. The yarns then pass through squeeze rollers to remove excess size, over the steam-heated cans to dry, through separator bars that break the yarns apart into individual yarns again and then wound onto warp beams. The yarn is now ready to be woven.

THE DENIM
MANUFACTURING PROCESS

5. Weaving

The indigo dyed warp yarns are interlaced with the natural colored weft yarns during this process. This is achieved by individually controlling each of the warp yarns, so that a portion is raised and a portion is lowered to form an opening called a "shed." The weaving takes place by the insertion of the weft yarn into the shed by means of a small projectile, a jet of air or a rapier, depending on the type of machine used. After each insertion, or "pick," the yarn is cut to produce the fringe at the edge of the fabric. On modern weaving equipment, the same warp thread can be continuously woven for more than 2,000 yards.

Workers in Cone Denim's White Oak Plant Weave Room in 1909. Photograph provided by Cone Denim.

THE DENIM
MANUFACTURING PROCESS

Vintage Shuttle Weaving The major difference between modern looms and vintage shuttle looms is that the weft insertion is accomplished by the use of a "shuttle" that carries the weft yarn from one end to the other. In addition, the ends are not cut after each pick, which is what forms the "selvage" edge (self edge). While modern looms usually produce denim that is between 58" to 62", vintage shuttle looms are traditionally only about 28" to 31" in width.

6. Finishing

The final processes performed on woven denim fabric include "Sanforizing" (pre-shrinking), surface texturing and "skewing," which is a process first applied by Cone Denim to prevent the twisting of the legs of garments during sewing.

Rolls of denim being inspected at the White Oak Plant, 1909.   Photograph provided by Cone Denim.

INSPIRATION

The beauty of denim is partly due to its ever changing facade. As it is constantly aging and degrading, softening and fading, a well worn pair of denim will rarely look the same on its last days, as it did on its first. While denim's outward appearance continues to change, its overall utility and usefulness, on par with the most reliable of tools, remains. Even when its original form is no longer recognizable, denim maintains its value as it ends up as vital patching material used to prolong the life of other pairs in the wearer's collection.

The rare images that follow are examples of some of the oldest surviving authentic vintage denim in existence. Most now call home the secure vaults and archives of some America's original denim pioneers: LS&CO., Lee, and Cone Denim.

As you let these images soak in, try to imagine what the wearer did for a living. What kind of climate, exposure and substances did they come in contact with on a daily basis, and what were the potential causes of the rips, tears, repairs, stains and fading?

After studying these images, you may never look at denim jeans in the same way again.

The "XX" Jean

The "XX", c1879, is the oldest known 501® jean in existence. This jean was made just 6 years after the first riveted blue jean was produced by LS&CO. in 1873. When the original owner was wearing these jeans, Edison had just invented the electric lamp.

Courtesy Levi Strauss & Co. Archives, San Francisco.
Photo by Hangauer/Kissinger © 2005

The "XX" Jean

Courtesy Levi Strauss & Co. Archives, San Francisco.
Photo by Hangauer/Kissinger © 2005

The "Nevada Jean"

c1885. This pair of basic Levi's® riveted denim work pants, found in a Nevada mining town in the 1990's, features a left thigh ruler pocket, the pocket bags are denim, rather than twill, and the buttons have been sewn on by thread, rather than by use of shanks. LS&CO. purchased this piece of history for $46,532 on an Ebay auction in 2001.

Courtesy Levi Strauss & Co. Archives, San Francisco.
Photo by Hangauer/Kissinger © 2005

The "Nevada Jean"

Courtesy Levi Strauss & Co. Archives, San Francisco.
Photo by Hangauer/Kissinger © 2005

1890 501® Jean

This pair of 501® jeans was made in approximately 1890. Extensive repairs are visible, including an entire back pocket from another jean used to patch a large hole. The characteristic "spur bite" damage to the leg openings means their original owner was likely a cowboy.

Courtesy Levi Strauss & Co. Archives, San Francisco.

1890 501® Jean

Courtesy Levi Strauss & Co. Archives, San Francisco.

Boss of the Road Jean

c1900. This pair of Boss of the Road waist overalls features suspender buttons and back cinch. It was produced prior to the time belt loops were added to waist overalls.

Courtesy of Lee Jeans Archive.

Boss of the Road Jean

Courtesy of Lee Jeans Archive.

The Calico Mine Jean

This 501 jean, c1890, was found in the Calico Silver Mine in California's Mojave Desert in 1948.

Courtesy Levi Strauss & Co. Archives, San Francisco.

Lee Unionall

Lee Unionall's c1913.

Courtesy of Lee Jeans Archive.

The "Celebration Jean"

Originally purchased in 1917. The extensive patching was in reality padding apparently added by the original owner for protection. Underneath the 4 - 5 layers of denim padding, there are no holes or tears (other than on the back pockets). All of the original buttons have been replaced, with the exception of the waistband button, where a piece of twine has been threaded through the top buttonhole.

Courtesy Levi Strauss & Co. Archives, San Francisco.
Photo by Hangauer/Kissinger © 2005

The "Celebration Jean"

Courtesy Levi Strauss & Co. Archives, San Francisco.
Photo by Hangauer/Kissinger © 2005

Allen Waist Overall

Front & Back View of an Allen Waist Overall c1940. It has been converted by hand from a traditional overall to a waist-high overall. Although the original "Allen" button shanks are still present on the pockets, there are random suspender buttons on the waistband. The triangular suspender reinforcement is still intact on the back of the garment.

Photo courtesy of Cone Denim Archival Collection - Photograph by Christopher Clancy

Allen Waist Overall

Photo courtesy of Cone Denim Archival Collection - Photograph by Christopher Clancy

Big Winston Overall

Front & Back view of a Big Winston Overall made of Cone Deeptone Denim c1940. The original "Big Winston Overalls" buttons are still present. The missing back section on the left leg exposes the severe patching and repair this garment endured.

Photo courtesy of Cone Denim Archival Collection - Photograph by Christopher Clancy

Big Winston Overall

Photo courtesy of Cone Denim Archival Collection - Photograph by Christopher Clancy

1050's Lee Jean

Lee jeans c1950.

Courtesy of Lee Jeans Archive.

GETTING STARTED

There is no right or wrong way to finish your denim. It is an extremely personal endeavor. From the subtlest hint of abrasion on a seam to throwing the "kitchen sink" on your jeans, let each pair grow as an outlet of your creativity.

As your finishing skills grow, you will discover new applications for your tools, and new substances to replicate looks you admire. When working to replicate either an entire vintage style, or a specific finishing detail, it is helpful to give your task at hand sufficient thought before starting. Consider what the occupation was of the original owner. What type of work resulted in the specific wear patterns? What type of materials and substances were they exposed to on a daily basis? The answers to these questions will go a long way to helping you replicate the overall look and/or details.

GETTING STARTED

To help with inspiration, included throughout this book are rare images of some of the oldest surviving examples of true vintage denim work-wear from America. Study the wear patterns, stains, fading and numerous repairs these garments are carrying, and let them serve as your guide.

In addition to referencing these historical photos, we have provided a basic "Stain Guide" to help you select some of the most common substances to use in recreating particular staining techniques.

Please keep in mind that the art of finishing denim is just that, an art. Great art rarely happens quickly or spontaneously. It takes training and a great deal of time and patience to produce an artistic masterpiece, be it on canvas, on film, in music, or on a pair of denim jeans. The mediums may change, but the effort and dedication does not. Like everything worthwhile in life, you will get out of it what you put into it.

Please take note, we do NOT advocate the copying of any trade marked designs or otherwise protected intellectual property. On the contrary, the purpose of the Denim Design Lab™ is to provide a roadmap to help inspire you to use your own vision and creativity to both interpret what you see and discover new and unique finishing details.

Let's now take a look at some of the basic skills and techniques used to replicate vintage and other novelty denim.

THE DENIM DESIGN LAB™

If you are serious about customizing your denim and creating truly one of a kind works of wearable art, you will need access to the appropriate tools.

Available at only the most premium denim based retailers globally, the Denim Design Lab™ kit contains many of the most common tools of the trade used to hand finish denim.

The specific collection of tools contained in the DDL™ kit are designed to help create &/or accelerate an aged vintage appearance on store bought denim, rather than during the actual production process of denim (pre-retail).

Also included in the DDL™ kit is the exclusive DDL™ Denim Finishing Form™. The "DDL-DFF™" is an inflatable bladder that is inserted inside your jean to create a semi-firm work area to perform on. The DDL-DFF™ is a consumer version of what professional denim laundries actually use to finish jeans.

Each 100% hand-made denim kit is unique, and itself a work of art. No detail has been spared in the creation of the DDL™ kits. Collectors and aficionados will recognize and appreciate the level of detail built into each kit, and due to their extremely limited distribution, they will soon become the "must have" item for every true lover of denim.

The Denim Design Lab™ kits are produced from 100% Red Selvage denim from Cone Denim™, and hand finished by professional denim laundries. The initial release features three unique vintage inspired washes, each based on themes from the DDL™ book; the "Gold Miner," the "Painter," and the "Mechanic" as well as one "Raw" version.

The combination of the detailed "how to" section found in this book, combined with the Denim Design Lab™ kit, will help you add from subtle to extreme details to your denim to ensure you are wearing a one of a kind work of art.

THE DENIM DESIGN LAB™

Inside
"Mechanic" wash

Front
"Mechanic" wash

Back
"Gold Miner" wash

Also available in the "Painter" wash and "Raw"

Design • Detail • Create
Denim Design Lab™

TOOLS OF THE TRADE

Included with the Denim Design Lab™ Kit:

1. Denim Design Lab™ Book
2. Denim Design Lab™ Grinder
3. Denim Design Lab™ Grinding and Detailing Accessories:
    a. Belt Grinder
    b. Rounded Detail Sanding Bit
    c. Pointed Detail Sanding Bit
    d. Short Flat Detail Sanding Bit
    e. Medium Flat Detail Sanding Bit
    f. Dual Adjustment Wrench / Screwdriver
4. 180 Grit Wet/Dry Silicon Carbide Sandpaper
5. 1500 Grit Wet/Dry Silicon Carbide Sandpaper
6. Coarse Emery Sanding Cloth
7. Fine Emery Sanding Cloth
8. Denim Design Lab™ Seam Ripper
9. Inch/Metric Tape Measure
10. DDL™ Paint Brush
11. DDL™ Paint Dropper
12. DDL™ Spray Bottle
13. DDL™ Denim Finishing Form™
    (photo on following page)

Not Included with the Denim Design Lab™ Kit, but suggested:

1. Razor Knife
2. Tea Bags (preferably black or dark tea)
3. Sanding Block
5. Tag Gun w/ 1/4" plastic tags

TOOLS OF THE TRADE

Not Included with your Denim Design Lab™ Kit, but suggested:

6. Wire Brush
7. Wood Stains (see Stain Guide)
8. Acrylic Paints (see Stain Guide)
9. Oil Based Pastel Sticks (see Stain Guide)
10. Water Colors (see Stain Guide)
11. Bleach
12. Paint Thinner to clean your DDL™ Brush after each use

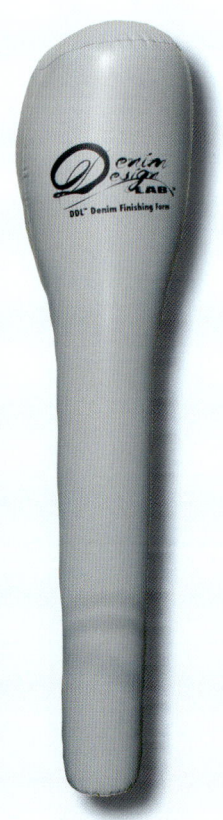

DDL™ Denim Finishing Form™

DESIGN · DETAIL · CREATE
The Art of Finishing Denim

Starting from "RAW"...

For those really looking to create a denim masterpiece, and who have the time to devote to the project, should start from a raw pair of denim jeans. Raw denim is rigid denim that has not yet been washed and treated. For denim design artists, raw denim is truly a blank canvas upon which anything is possible.

As raw denim will shrink like crazy, when deciding on the correct size to buy, remember that they will generally shrink 3 to 4 inches in length and about 2 inches around the waist. In addition, keep in mind that they will continue to shrink, if only slightly, during the first 3 washings. As such, we do not recommend altering the length (if you bought them too long) until at least after the third wash.

Levi's still sells great "shrink-to-fit" 501 jeans in raw rigid denim at affordable prices. These are your best bet for experimenting. If and when you are ready to go big, other more high-end options are raw Evisu's or G-Star's. Or, when you are really on top of your game, get your hands on some authentic Levi's vintage dead stock and start your masterpiece from one of the true originals.

STARTING FROM RAW

Ready to get started?

The first step is to actually put them on... and keep them on... as long as possible. Think of this experience as if you were trying to break in a wild horse; hard as hell, but ultimately extremely rewarding and worthwhile.

You should commit to wearing your raws' for at least three days straight to really kick-start the break-in process. After the second full day, while still wearing them, use your DDL™ Spray Bottle and lightly spray the areas around the thighs, crotch and behind the knees. Crouch down a few times, stretching the denim a bit, and accentuate the natural creases that should be forming in these areas. Repeat the light spraying again in these three areas.

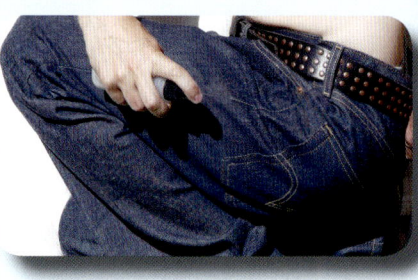

When these areas dry, the "whiskers" that are forming will be stiffer than the surrounding denim. Continue the above process once a day, if possible, for at least one week. Pick a hot day, and after your spraying routine, take your denim off and lay it out flat exposed to direct sunlight for as long as possible (don't forget to turn them over to expose the back of the knees as well). The above process will cause the target areas to fade slightly more than the surrounding areas.

Although subtle, the stiff ridges forming will provide you with an accurate guide of where to accentuate the natural whiskers. It is recommended that you highlight these areas prior to applying any general fading.

To accentuate the whiskering that you started with your DDL™ Spray Bottle routine, roll a small sheet of 1500 Grit Wet/Dry Silicon Carbide Sandpaper around a pen or pencil, and use scotch tape to secure the ends. The width of this "**whisker stick**" should be very close to that of the natural whiskers and wear marks that you have been nurturing up to this point.

Again using your Spray Bottle, moisten the areas you want to work on and then start to slowly run the stick along the line of the whisker. The more you rub, the more pronounced the wear marks become. Be careful not to get too carried away, if your whiskers are too pronounced compared to the overall color of your denim, it can start to look fake.

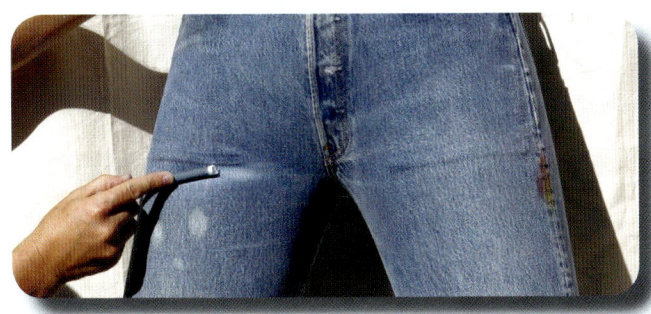

An alternative method for creating authentic looking whiskers is to use a sheet of 1500 or 180 Grit Wet/Dry Silicon Carbide Sandpaper (use dry). With the sandpaper wrapped around only one fingertip, slowly apply subtle pressure along the ridges of the stiff creases until you achieve a subtle, but noticeable fade. With additional fading over the entire thigh, crotch and area behind the knees, the whiskers will start to blend in and look natural.

Before   After

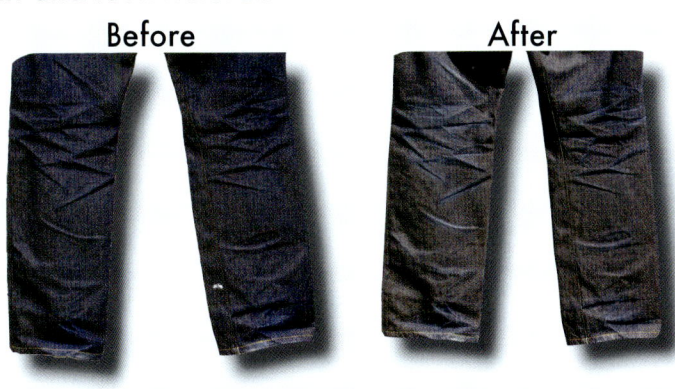

STARTING FROM RAW

After

At this point, your raw denim is still very dark, but softening up by the day. Depending on what the ultimate look is for this pair, you will either be good to go, or may you have only just begun your journey to the perfect pair of jeans.

If you want them to remain as dark as possible, wash them as little as possible, and when you do, do so by hand and with either little or no soap or detergent. Always turn them inside out to help prevent fading. If you are trying to lighten them up, the more they are exposed to warm water and harsh detergents (especially those containing bleach), the faster they will continue to fade.

If you intend to create any "resin bake creases" on this pair, it is a good idea to set them up prior to exposure to the sun &/or washing them for the first time. Instructions for achieving this particular effect are discussed on pg. 108; skip ahead before continuing work on this pair.

To achieve greater fading over larger areas, such as the thigh area, use a sheet of either 180 Grit Wet/Dry Silicon Carbide Sandpaper or Coarse Emery Sanding Cloth and steadily work the area to lightly abrade and fade to your desired shade. Misting the area first with a light layer of water mixed with approximately 10% - 20% bleach will hasten the process and cause more fading with less abrasion.

Once you are happy with the overall look of your "masterpiece in progress,"...

STARTING FROM RAW

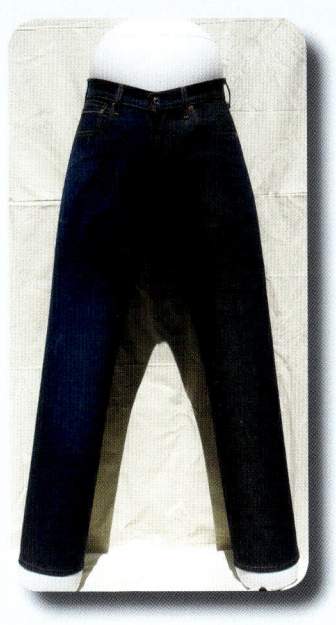
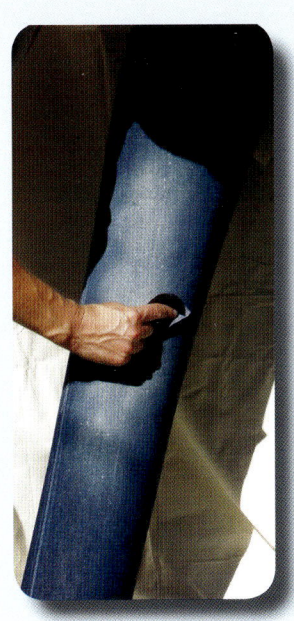

It is time to get into the details

If you have followed the general advice offered so far, you should now have a good base to start from for further detailing. While the starch that was in your original raw denim has likely been washed and/or rubbed out by this time, the natural wear and whiskering marks you have created will be your guidepost to help you focus on the key areas for further work.

Using your Denim Design Lab™ Grinder, with the DDL™ Belt Grinder, rough up the hem, seams, belt loops, back pockets, over stitching, waist band, and front pockets to achieve an authentic worn out look. Review the chapters on abrasion and grinding for details and photos for each of these target areas, and the chapter on staining to add the final touches to your one of a kind denim masterpiece.

If you did not start with a raw garment, and will be working on a pair with pre-existing wear and fading, you can start from here to learn how to further fade and accentuate the existing finish on your denim, or create entirely new finishing details.

STARTING FROM RAW

After

Before

FADING

Tools

TARGET AREAS: Front & back of thighs, knees & seat.

BACKGROUND: Especially with raw and new dark denim, fading is the most widely used finishing process. Fading can be very subtle, causing the softening up of the denim with little change in color, all the way to 100% elimination of the indigo (bleached out). Fading concerns the lightening in color, and not abrasion (which is also a by-product of fading when using sand paper). Abrasion will be reviewed in the next chapter.

HOW TO:
Fading large areas of raw or very dark denim is best accomplished when you start with a sheet of Coarse Emery Sanding Cloth (included in your DDL™ Kit). Once you begin to achieve a shade close to your target, switch to a sheet of Fine Emery Sanding Cloth, and then, after lightly misting your target areas with water from your DDL™ Spray Bottle, move to a sheet of 1500 Grit Wet/Dry Silicon Carbide Sandpaper to fine tune your fade.

For best results, you should sand in the same direction as the grain in the fabric (i.e., following the indigo warp yarns), and only perpendicular to the warp to help shave off fuzz generated from sanding.

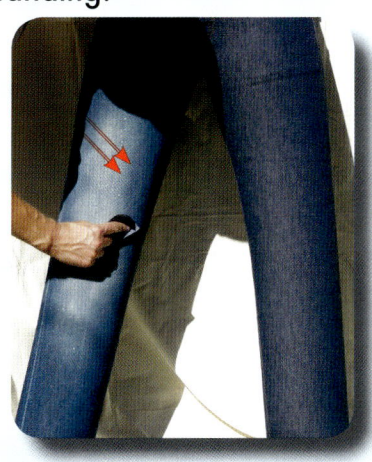

FADING

Be careful to secure the area of your jeans you will be working on so that the denim does not move, gather or bunch up. Using large clips to secure the pair to your work area will help keep your target area flat and allow for even fading without unwanted wear lines (from the fabric moving while sanding).

By far the most efficient way to work on large areas such as these is to put your pair of jeans on a Denim Design Lab™ Denim Finishing Form™ ("DDL-DFF") (photo below). The surface area will be smooth, yet with enough give to ensure you are able to achieve a great fade with sanding.

For comparison, note the difference between the left and right legs on this work in progress.

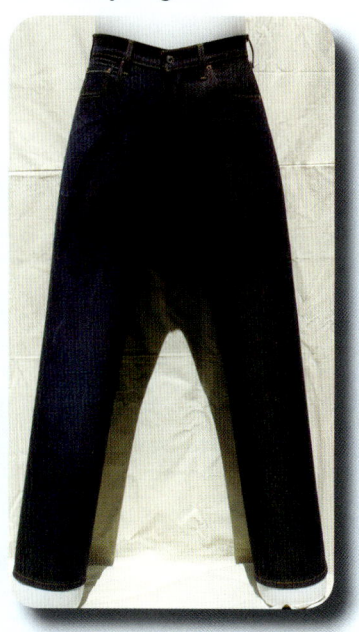

FADING

To hasten the fading process, you can spray the target areas with a mixture of water with between 10% to 20% bleach before or after hand sanding. This will speed up the fading, and limit the amount of sanding required to achieve a good fade. However, be very careful with the use of bleach.

Always start with a low concentration of bleach to water, and allow it to sit while exposed to the sun for at least 10 minuets, before judging the outcome of the fade. Starting with too much bleach &/or continuing before it drys can result in over bleaching your denim. Remember... you can always add more, but you can't go back once you spray the bleach mix. Always test your mixture on a scrap of denim before proceeding on your actual pair.

This image shows the level of fading after the spraying of a 20% bleach mixture to the thigh and waist areas of the left leg. The right side has been left raw.

ABRASION

Tools

TARGET AREAS: Front & back of thighs, calfs, pockets, knees & seat.

BACKGROUND: After fading, abrasion detailing is by far the most common finishing technique. From subtle wear marks to huge holes, abrasion details cheat time and allow you to create the look of age and abuse in minutes or hours, rather than months and years.

Abrasion details fall into one of three broad categories: light abrasion, wear holes and "white holes." For all types, if you will be using your Denim Design Lab™ Grinder in combination with your DDL™ Denim Finishing Form™, be sure to insert a small piece of thick paper or cardboard between your denim and your DDL™ DFF™ at the target work area(s) to ensure you do not puncture your DFF™.

ABRASION

HOW TO:

Light Abrasion

If you have an idea of the shape you want your abrasion pattern to end up, you can lightly draw the shape on your denim with a crayon or other nonpermanent marking device (you can sand it off as you work). Start with a sheet of 1500 Grit Wet/Dry Silicon Carbide Sandpaper and slowly begin abrading your target area(s). Once you begin to achieve a shade close to your target, lightly mist the area(s) with water from your DDL™ Spray Bottle and continue to fine tune to your desired shade.

Wear Holes

To create authentic looking small wear holes, start by cutting a small nick at your target location with a razor knife. You can use either your Fine Emery Sanding Cloth or a wire brush to open the hole a bit and create some loose threads. Again, be sure to sand down the surrounding area a bit to help avoid too much contrast. A wire brush is recommended for opening up larger, more uneven holes, as it is a way more aggressive tool then sand paper. Be extremely careful when using your DDL™ DFF™ with either a razor knife or wire brush, due to the possibility of a puncture taking place.

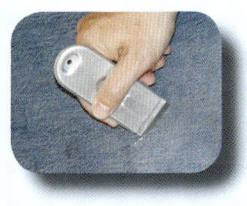 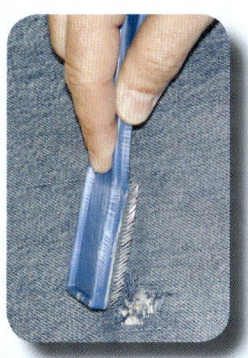 

ABRASION

"White Holes"

To create "white holes," start by slightly sanding down an area roughly twice the size of the white hole you want to end up with. This is necessary to ensure the hole looks like it occurred naturally. If the surrounding area is too clean and untouched, your hole will look fake and out of place.

Once you have roughed up your target area, use your razor knife to slowly scrape away just the indigo dyed warp yarns (that run vertically down your jeans) to expose the underlying white weft, or filling yarns. As you see the white yarns start to appear, slow down your scraping so you do not to accidentally rip too many of these filling yarns. For best results, always scrape in the direction of the indigo warp threads. Be extremely careful when using your DDL™ DFF™ with a razor knife, due to the possibility of a puncture taking place.

 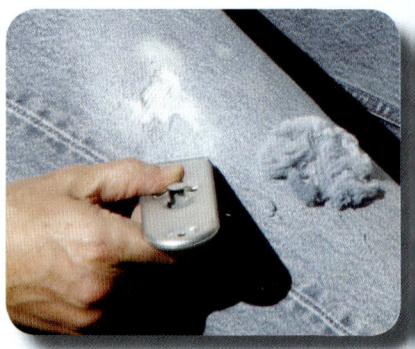

To give your "white hole" an aged appearance, use your DDL™ Spray Bottle and spray some "Tea Stain" over the hole and surrounding area. See the chapter on Tinting, pg. 104.

GRINDING

Tools

TARGET AREAS: Hem, seams, belt loops, back pockets, over stitching, waistband and front pockets.

BACKGROUND: As with abrasion detailing, grinding allows you to create the look of age and abuse. Your Denim Design Lab Grinder™ is the ultimate tool for fine-tuning your denim.

If you will be using your Denim Design Lab™ Grinder in combination with your DDL™ Denim Finishing Form™, be sure to insert a small piece of thick paper or cardboard between the denim and your DDL™ DFF™ at the target work area(s) to ensure you do not puncture your DFF™.

HOW TO:

Pick the Best Attachment for your Target Area
Depending on the size of your target grinding area, particular DDL™ grinding attachments are recommended.

To achieve an authentic worn out look, start with the DDL™ Belt Grinder attachment. The DDL™ Belt Grinder is the most aggressive of your DDL™ attachments and will quickly grind down your target areas. With this attachment, you can easily create wear holes or "spur bites" in your cuffs, grind holes in the waistband, coin pocket or other target areas, and generally "destroy" your denim if you are looking for an extremely worn / abused look. The DDL™ Belt Grinder attachment is best used on target areas larger than 1/2".

Be careful with this attachment, as you can easily create holes where you may not intend them if you grind too fast. With this attachment, it is recommended to keep your DDL™ Grinder on a low spin speed (3 - 5), unless you are really trying to create a hole or grind down (or off) a belt loop in a hurry.

GRINDING

To get into smaller areas and/or fine sand, either the DDL™ Rounded or Pointed Detail Sanding Bits are recommended. With your DDL™ Grinder on a medium setting, carefully highlight areas in between double stitch lines and belt loops, strategically remove stitching, and work individual threads to create detailed wear marks.

The DDL™ Short Flat and Medium Flat Detail Sanding Bits are ideal for larger surface areas where you need a flat surface area worn. Along the outer seam of the legs on your jeans, run either of these attachments, at medium speed, to help bring out "train tracks" or contrast lines from the underlining selvage or seam.

GRINDING

SHOW THROUGH WEAR MARKS

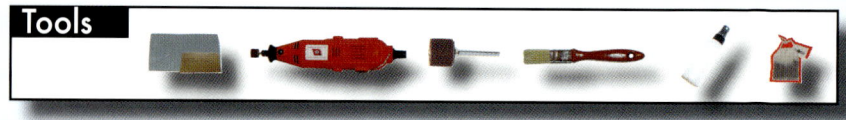

Tools

TARGET AREAS: Back pockets, front coin/watch pocket.

BACKGROUND: Years of repeated wear causes objects kept in a particular pocket to create a visible outline and begin to wear through in places. One of the most common wear-through patterns found in vintage denim is the "tobacco tin," however, wallets, lighters and coins all work great.

HOW TO:
Place your wallet (or any similarly shaped / sized object) in the pocket. Using a sheet of 1500 Grit Wet/Dry Silicon Carbide Sandpaper, lightly sand around the edges of the wallet until you achieve just enough fading that the outline begins to appear.

SHOW THROUGH WEAR MARKS

To create more extreme looking wear, continue to sand in one or two small areas with the sand paper until you begin to break through the denim, creating small holes. To create these holes quicker, you can also use your Denim Design Lab™ Grinder with the Belt Grinder attachment.

For additional detailing, brush a small amount of **wood stain or water color** on a section of the outline, to create a dirty / stained effect. Be careful not to make the stain too even looking.

To further age this area, use your DDL™ Spray Bottle filled with a brew of one or more bags of dark / black tea. If you only want the area of the impression to be stained, use some masking tape to cover the surrounding area before spraying. After lightly spraying this area, let the jean sit in the hot sun for an hour or two to dry and help the tea stain set in.

VARIATIONS:

Using the same process as above for back pockets, you can customize your front coin pocket using smaller items. Try coins, a key or key chain.

For a different effect, spray or rub a small amount of diluted bleach (approximately 30% bleach, 70% water) either just over the outline, or over a the entire pocket, to create a layered stain.

TINTING

Tools: 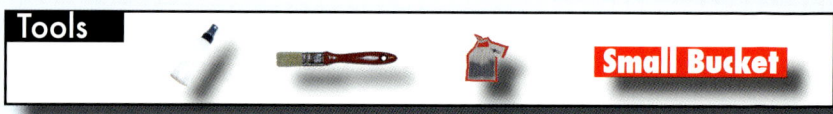 Small Bucket

TARGET AREAS: Over rips, thigh, knee and seat area, "all over."

BACKGROUND: You can create an antiqued "dirty denim" looking tint with the help of some common tea bags and water. On vintage denim that has been exposed to years of harsh elements and perspiration, you will often find a similar tint as the indigo color takes on a slight light brown cast resembling a tea stain.

HOW TO:
To give specific wear areas a slightly aged appearance, fill your DDL™ Spray Bottle with a brew of dark or black tea and mist over the target area until moist. Exposing the treated areas to direct sunlight will help set the stain. Repeat process until you achieve the desired color. Experiment with different types of tea to achieve varying tints.

If you are working on tinting a larger surface area of your denim, be sure to apply varying amounts of your "Tea-Tint" to certain areas based on where you would expect the most fading to occur naturally. For larger areas, you can also use your DDL™ Paint Brush to apply a good coat.

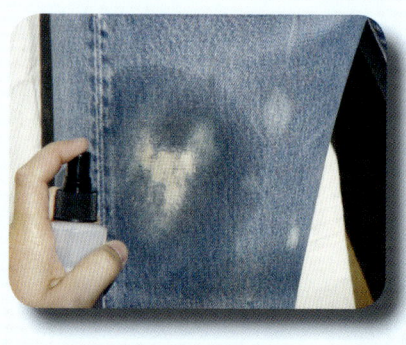

TINTING

A second round of sanding / spraying / sun exposure will help ensure your work is not too uniform looking. It is always a good idea to have a target sample next to you to help identify the locations and severity of fading to replicate an authentic look.

You can also use a "Tea-Tint" to over-dye your entire garment. In a small bucket (photo), add approximately 12 large tea bags to warm water, stir and let sit for approximately 30 minutes.

Before throwing your denim in there, be sure to test a scrape piece to ensure you are happy with the shade it produces. Add more water or tea bags as needed to achieve the tint you are trying to achieve. The longer you leave your denim in there, the darker the tint will be. Again, always test first.

Before   After

STAINING

TARGET AREAS: Over rips, pockets, thighs, over seams, "random".

BACKGROUND: Using your DDL™ Dropper and/or DDL™ Brush, you can apply a variety of common substances to your denim to replicate both industrial and natural stains often found on vintage denim. Reference the Stain Guide starting on pg. 120 to help you identify colors, tints and products to create each of the below finishing effects.

HOW TO:

Bleach. The most common bleach stains are drips and drops. To control the size and shade of the bleach stain, we recommend using your DDL™ Dropper. To stain larger areas, use your DDL™ Brush to apply stokes of bleach. With this technique, you can bleach out an entire coin pocket as in the below photo.

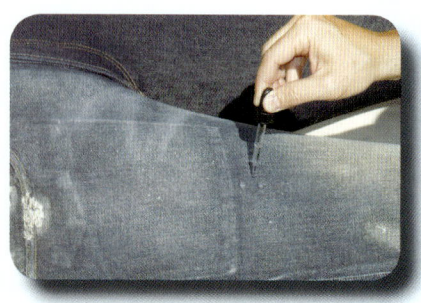

Be sure to test the size and color of the stain that will be created prior to starting on your actual denim. When preparing your mixture, remember the higher the concentration of bleach, the whiter the stain. Consult the Stain Guide to help confirm the fade you want to achieve.

STAINING

Industrial Stains. Various shades of wood stain are great for replicating industrial stains such as oil or grease, if you don't mind a textured appearance. To avoid texture, use water color. Use your DDL™ Brush to apply the stain to seams, near pockets and thigh area. An old dish rag can also be used to rub the stain on to achieve a more erratic, naturally occurring stain.

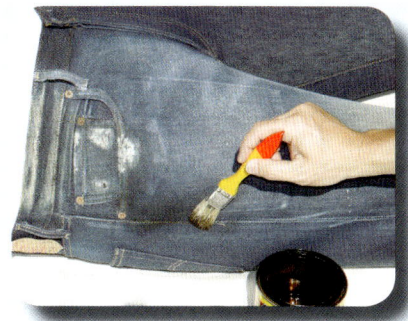 

Paint. Paint stains can either be dripped on or brushed on to cover a larger surface area. Use your DDL™ Brush to apply one or multiple colors to seams, near pockets and thigh area.

To recreate the look of an accidental run in with the top of a paint or wood stain can, simply coat the inside rim of the can with paint or other stain, turn it over and apply to your back pocket, thigh or other area. Be sure not to make it look too even; apply varying amounts of paint / stain around the rim, and do not apply the same amount of pressure to all sides when stamping your denim. If you will use this technique often, you can take a wooden dowel and secure it to the top with a nail. Using a file, you can erode some of the outside rim of the can top to ensure your stamps have an uneven look.

RESIN BAKE CREASES

Tools

TARGET AREAS: Waistband, top of front pockets, back pockets and cuffs.

BACKGROUND: "Resin Bake" Creases are a relatively new finishing treatment, usually found on higher-end denim styles. The process seeks to replicate the look of permanent creases which normally would occur only after repeated wear and abuse heaped on specific areas. Staining is sometimes associated with these creases.

In traditional denim laundries, this expensive technique usually entails the use of an industrial resin that is brushed or sprayed on the target area and then "baked" under high heat to activate the resin and set the crease.

Denim Design Lab™ uses the below techniques to achieve a similar look, without the use of resin or an industrial oven.

HOW TO:
Using a Tag Gun and short 1/4" tags, pinch together 2 to 3 folds of denim, of about one to three inches in length, and secure them with enough tags so that each section is touching the next without any spaces in between. The area should be secure enough to withstand some finishing abuse. If you do not have access to a Tag Gun, you can use metal document clips as a back-up.

"RESIN BAKE" CREASES

If you are adding this treatment to a raw or very dark garment, you will be able to achieve a good deal of contrast, as the protected portions will remain much darker than the surrounding areas you are working on. For unwashed shrink-to-fit jeans, it is a good idea to keep the target area(s) tagged for the first week of wear, and if possible, until after the first wash. Be sure to mist these areas with your spray bottle after the second day of wear, and at least once each day after that. Leave them out to bake in the sun after about the third day to help ensure that the ridges set. The starch in your raw denim will help the creases stay in place after you spray them with water.

For all shades of denim, be sure to lightly sand down the top of the ridges as well as the area surrounding the tagged portion(s) with 1500 Grit Wet/Dry Silicon Carbide Sandpaper to rough-up, fade and increase the overall contrast of these details. For lighter, more worn looking shades, you can incorporate more severe abrasion next to the creased areas with your DDL™ Belt Grinder attachment for a really vintage abused look.

To add further contrast, the creased areas can be sprayed with a batch of "tea stain" to give it an aged appearance. Lightly brushing some varnish or wood stain over the area will not only create a stained effect, but permanently set the creases as well.

"RESIN BAKE" CREASES

1. Pinch together two to three layers and either clip them together (pictured) or secure with multiple plastic tags.

2. Lightly sand down the tops and surrounding area around the ridges.

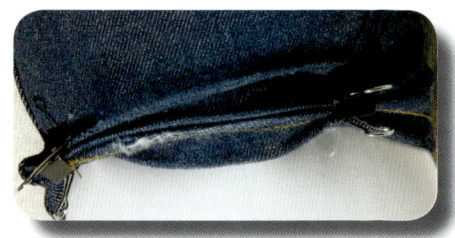

3. Spray or rub a small amount of bleach (20%) around the creased ares (if heavy fading is desired).

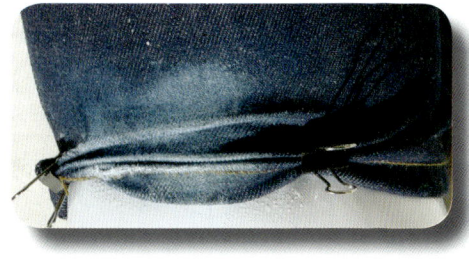

4. Take off the clips or remove the tags to view your new "resin bake creases."

5. Add some "Tea Stain" or other staining, with some additional grinding at the cuff, to finish off the job.

HEM ALTERATIONS

Tools

TARGET AREAS: Cuffs.

BACKGROUND: If you hem a pair of pre-finished and/or worn jeans, rather than rolling them at the cuff, you will be left with a cuff that is likely very out of place compared to the rest of your garment. Your DDL™ Kit can help you quickly bring this alteration in line with the rest of the jean.

HOW TO:
First off, try to have the altered cuff sewn using real 100% cotton denim thread in as close a color as the rest of the thread used. Whenever possible, try to ensure a chain stitch is used (as was likely used on the original). The reason for this is that the combination of 100% cotton thread and a chain stitch create a very unique look when they shrink. The cuff will be full of small waves and ridges with lots of contrast caused by the shrinkage.

After hemming, be sure to roughen up the front, back and top of the cuff with your Fine Emery Sanding Cloth, and if the overall look of the denim is more worn and vintage, use your DDL™ Belt Grinder attachment to wear some small holes as shown below. You can also spray some "Tea Stain" around the entire cuff area to simulate an aged appearance.

ADVANCED TECHNIQUES

These techniques allow you to supercharge your denim. From extreme patching to replicate substantial age and wear, to embellishments that add a more modern personal twist, the addition of one or more of the following techniques can give an old pair of plain basic denim the ultimate face lift.

EMBELLISHMENTS

BACKGROUND: Once you have the basic denim design skills down and are ready to explore embellishment options, you can try adding some of these finishing touches to your masterpiece. One of the hottest trends returning to today's high-end denim market is the addition of patches, crystals, embroidery, beading, heavy thread over-stitching and studs. With the exception of embroidery (unless you happen to have an embroidery machine in your garage...), you can recreate many of these looks with an array of readily available trim.

HOW TO: Studding

Tools		
Metal Studs	Stud Setter	

TARGET AREAS: Back pockets, top of front pockets, belt loops, "random".

If you will be creating a specific design, start by making a template. Draw the outline on a sheet of paper, and keeping in mind the size of the studs you will be using, place a dot in the center of where each one will be placed. Secure your template on the target area of your denim with scotch tape, and then make small guide holes using the tip of your DDL™ Seam Ripper. Remove your template, and begin applying the studs with a stud setter (available where you purchased your studs). For added effect, you can stitch around the outline of your shape with some thick thread.

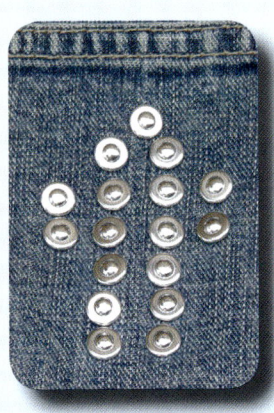

EMBELLISHMENTS

HOW TO: Hand Stitch Detailing

Tools: Heavy Thread | Needle & Thread

TARGET AREAS: Back pockets, top of front pockets, belt loops, "random".

These are great for adding contrast color pop to your denim and can vary from a simple thick yarn loop stitch over the edge of a pocket or belt loop, to a more elaborately stitched design placed over a pocket or elsewhere on the denim. For graphic elements, first sketch the design on a piece of paper to map out the colors. Once you are happy with it, use a thin marker to create the pattern directly on your denim as a guide for your stitches.

For added detail, apply a cut-to-shape piece of adhesive felt or other contrast fabric to your target area prior to applying the stitches. The dual fabrications will give this detail both depth and added texture (photo, bottom right).

RIP N' REPAIR

BACKGROUND:
If you do not have a sewing machine, you can still accomplish these distinctive aging features by hand or by taking the raw materials to your local tailor to finish. On the most basic level, Rip n' Repair detailing entails the simple patching of holes, either from the top or underneath, with a spare piece of denim or other fabric.

HOW TO: Underlay Stitch Repairs

Tools		
	Sewing Machine	Fusing

TARGET AREAS: Thighs, cuffs, knees.

Stitch repairs use a base of thin fabric or fusing behind the hole or extreme abrasion to add support for the overlay of multiple stitches. In vintage denim, you will often find multiple stitch repairs, usually with contrast thread color, that were made to keep the holes from spreading or ripping open. Start from an existing wear mark or hole or create a new one. Cut a scrap of fabric or fusing that covers the shape of your repair with an additional 1/4" to 1/2" to spare on all ends. Position this piece directly under your target and single stitch it to the denim. Once secure, the goal is to run as many additional stitches as possible to create a solid surface where the whole was.

Back side of patch showing fusing

RIP N' REPAIR

HOW TO: Contrast fabric underlay patches

Tools: Needle & Thread | Fabric or Patch Material

TARGET AREAS: Thighs, cuffs, knees.

Bandanas and other printed or solid woven materials, sewn underneath holes of various sizes, create great contrast and color interest on your denim. Rather than just a repair, these are seen as an additional design element on your denim. Cut a scrap of fabric that covers the shape of your repair with an additional 1/2" to 1" to spare on all sides. Position this piece directly under your target and run a few rows of single stitching along the edges of the hole to secure the patch. Unlike with an underlay repair, you do not have to cover the surface of the fabric, just ensure it is secured to the denim. Use a contrasting pop thread color to add additional interest, or try to match the base color of the denim if you want your patch to be the only source of contrast. Various qualities and shades of denim can also be used as the underlying repair material, and will add further contrast as the two fabrics fade and wear differently. Iron-on patch repair material can also be used in place of fabric / stitching.

Back side of iron-on patch

RIP N' REPAIR

HOW TO: Denim overlay repairs

Tools 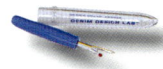 **Needle & Thread**

TARGET AREAS: Thighs, cuffs, knees.

These are basically your old school "Buster Brown" looking patches. Rather then sewing the patch underneath the hole, these are placed directly over the target area on top of your denim. They can be secured by fabric glue or with a couple of rows of stitching. To add more interest, the stitching can be made more erratic and zigzag over the edge of the patch and onto the denim. Again, using various qualities and shades of denim for the patch will ensure further contrast as the two fabrics will fade and wear differently.

HOW TO: Re-Engineered Repairs

Tools   **Needle & Thread**

TARGET AREA: Cuffs.

For a more extreme and experimental look, try re-engineering sections of your denim. Start with a pair of jeans that is at least 2" longer than needed after being washed, shrunk and hemmed. Measure and mark the length that the finished jean should be (allowing for seam allowance, etc.). Open up the seam approximately 6" with your DDL™ Seam Ripper. Cut the excess fabric at the cuff and turn it inside out. Re-sew and finish. Or, use a section of the cut excess, inside out, (or denim from another jean, in a different shade and quality) and insert it in between the upper part of the jean and a section of the original cuff. Experiment with different placements and fabrications.

PROJECT GALLERY

The "Jr. Painter"

Levi's® 550® w/ fading, painting & staining

The "Jr. Mechanic"

Levi's® 550® w/ fading, abrasion, grinding & staining

PROJECT GALLERY

The "Mechanic"

Raw Levi's® 501® w/ fading, abrasion, grinding & staining

The "BT Special"

Hand painted Oakley® jean w/ bleach, screen & overdye by Brian Takumi

STAIN GUIDE

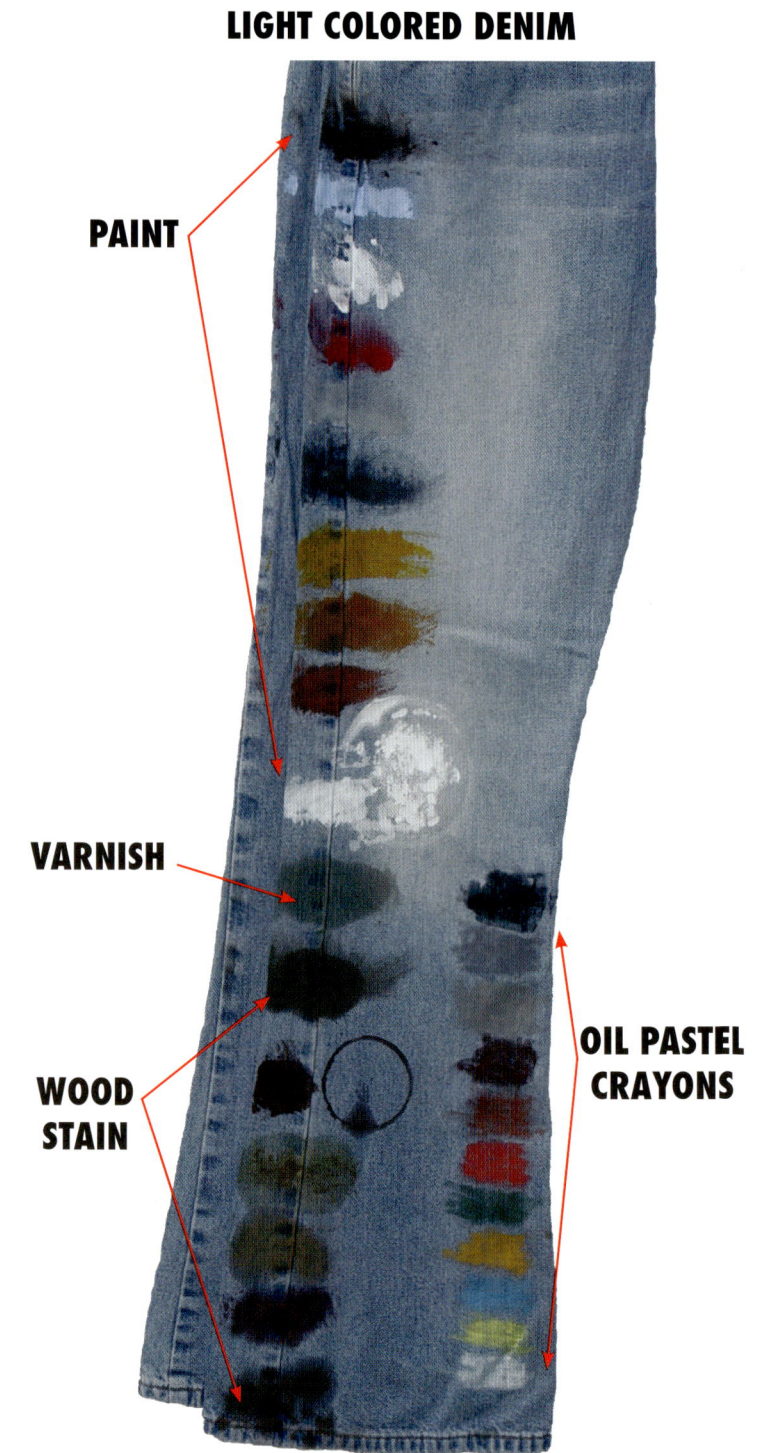

LIGHT COLORED DENIM

PAINT

VARNISH

WOOD STAIN

OIL PASTEL CRAYONS

STAIN GUIDE

DARK COLORED DENIM

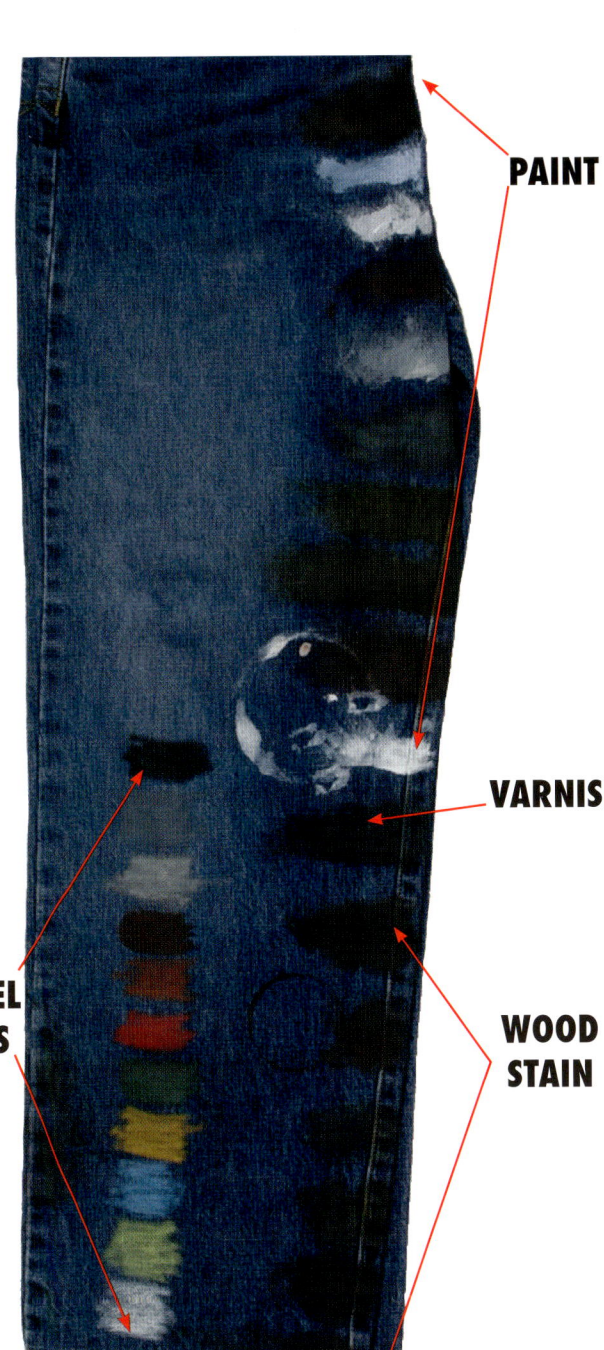

STAIN GUIDE

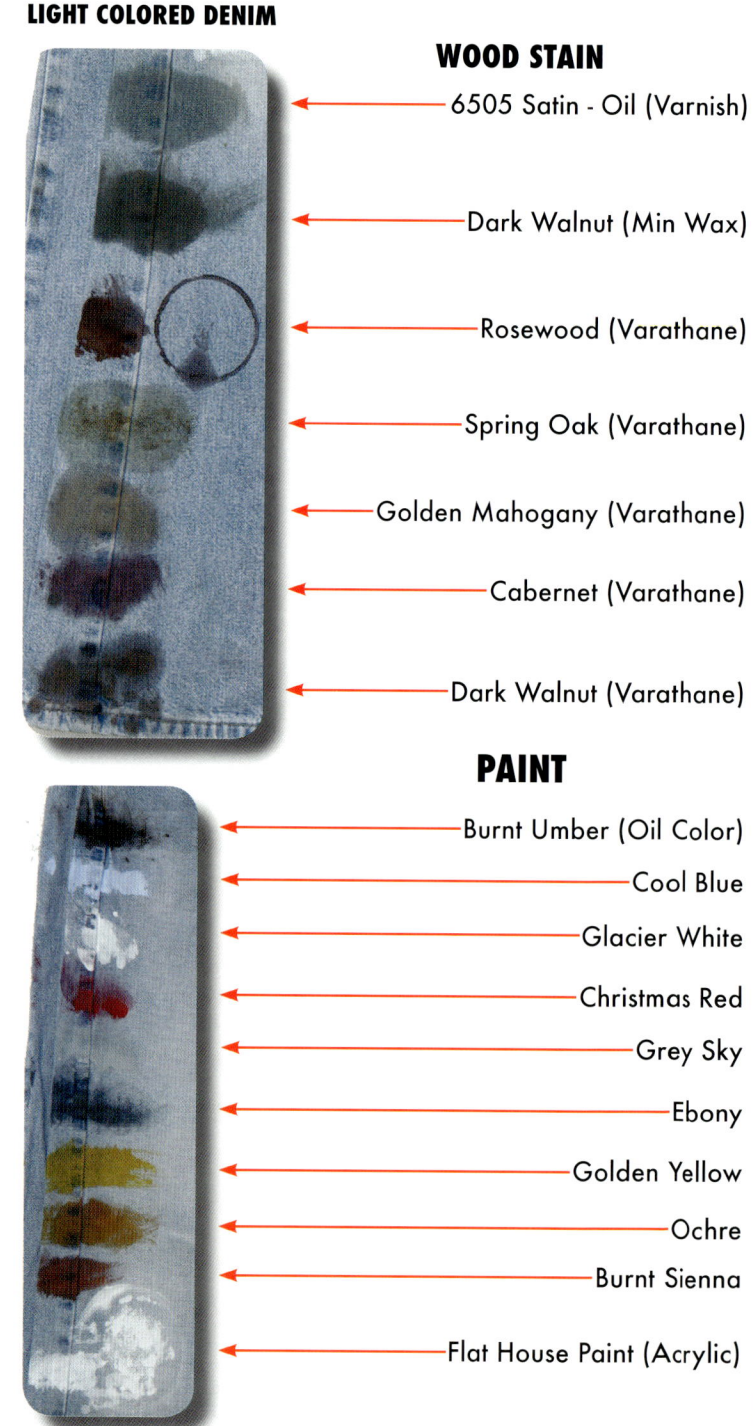

LIGHT COLORED DENIM

WOOD STAIN

- 6505 Satin - Oil (Varnish)
- Dark Walnut (Min Wax)
- Rosewood (Varathane)
- Spring Oak (Varathane)
- Golden Mahogany (Varathane)
- Cabernet (Varathane)
- Dark Walnut (Varathane)

PAINT

- Burnt Umber (Oil Color)
- Cool Blue
- Glacier White
- Christmas Red
- Grey Sky
- Ebony
- Golden Yellow
- Ochre
- Burnt Sienna
- Flat House Paint (Acrylic)

STAIN GUIDE

DARK COLORED DENIM

WOOD STAIN

- 6505 Satin - Oil (Varnish)
- Dark Walnut (Min Wax)
- Rosewood (Varathane)
- Spring Oak (Varathane)
- Golden Mahogany (Varathane)
- Cabernet (Varathane)
- Dark Walnut (Varathane)

PAINT

- Burnt Umber (Oil Color)
- Cool Blue
- Glacier White
- Christmas Red
- Grey Sky
- Ebony
- Golden Yellow
- Ochre
- Burnt Sienna
- Flat House Paint (Acrylic)

STAIN GUIDE

OIL PASTEL CRAYONS

- Black
- Dark Grey
- Pink Grey
- Van Dyke Brown
- Burnt Sienna
- Cadmium Red
- Lime Green
- Golden Ochre
- Light Blue
- Lemon Yellow
- White

BLEACH

- 100%
- 50%
- 20%
- 10%
- 80%
- 50%
- 20%
- 10%

STAIN GUIDE

WATER COLORS

Bluish Black, Sepia, Stone Gray, Medium Gray, Beige, Coffee Brown

Water colors are your best bet for recreating authentic industrial stains, and unlike with wood stains, they do not produce any noticeable texture. Using the supplied dropper, mix one dropper full of color to two to three droppers full of water in a mixing dish (as in above photo). Concentrated water colors mix incredibly well together, so depending on the exact stain you are trying to replicate, you can mix any number of colors together to achieve your stain. In general, the more water that is added, the lighter and more translucent your stain will be. Using pure or only slightly diluted stain is good for oil, grease and other dark stains, whereas more watered down colors are good for adding more subtle tints and light stains to your denim.

Glossary of Denim Terms

Abrasion
Process of making garments look worn and aged by scraping or rubbing the surface of the fabric causing abrasion. Pumice stones are most frequently used by industrial laundries (see Stone Washing). You can use your Denim Design Lab Rotary Tool and sand paper to replicate this process.

Acid Wash
(Marble Wash/Moon Wash/Snow Wash) - This finish gives indigo jeans sharp contrasts. The process is achieved by soaking pumice stones in chlorine and letting these stones create contrast. The process was created in Italy and patented in 1986.

Aka-Mimi
See "Selvage."

Atari
A Japanese term describing the selective fading of the ridges of creases. The most common areas for "Atari" are along side seams, on the front and back of the knees, the upper thigh, along the hem, on belt loops and along pocket seams. Your Denim Design Lab is designed to help you create "Atari." See also "Whiskering."

Bartak
A sewing procedure that reinforces stress points on jeans. – Usually found near zippers and pocket openings.

Beam
In the denim manufacturing process, a beam refers to a cylinder on which warp yarns are wound for further processing.

GLOSSARY CONT.

Big E
Refers to Levi's jeans produced prior to 1971. Up to that time, the name "LEVI'S" was written in all capital letters on the red "tab device" sewn into the back pocket. After this time, the "e" was written in lower case; "LeVI'S." Levi's jeans with a big E are considered vintage and more valuable than latter "little e's."

Bleach
A chemical used to make denim fade. Liquid bleach is usually an aqueous solution of sodium hypochlorite, and dry powdered bleaches contain chloride of lime (calcium hypochlorite).

Broken Twill
A denim weave first used by Wrangler in 1964, as style 13MWZ. The diagonal weave of the twill is intentionally reversed at every two warp ends to form a random design. This type of weave reduces the natural torque characteristic of regular twill weaves, and has the effect of eliminating leg twist.

Bull Denim
A 3X1 twill weave piece dyed fabric made of course yarns; weights can very from 9 ounces per square yard up to the standard 14 ounces per square yard. Basically, denim without indigo.

Cast
A term that describes shading. Depending on the method and type of dye used, indigo denim can have a black, brown, gray, green, red or yellow cast to it.

Cellulose Enzyme Wash
Enzymes, which are like yeast, are used to physically eat away the cellulose in cotton. Since the color in denim fabric is actually on the outside of the yard, when denim is washed in a cellulose enzyme bath the indigo is removed along with the fiber. When the desired color has been achieved, either

changing the alkalinity of the bath or heating the water stops the enzymes from reacting. A rinsing and softening cycle follows. This process is more environmentally friendly than stone washing because strip-mined pumice stones are not used.

Crocking
A term used to describe how dye rubs off fabric on skin or other fabric. Because indigo is on the surface of the yarn, color transfer is an issue manufacturers must contend with for denim fabrics. A resin or fixative provides resistance to rubbing or crocking, especially with medium to dark shades of denim. In addition, a water-repellent finish can also help prevent color loss.

Crosshatch
A unique type of denim that shows a square grid-like pattern in the weave. It is created by mixing uneven yarns in both the weft and warp directions.

Denim
A cotton fabric (traditionally 100% cotton, but can now be found blended with other fibers), made with indigo dyed warp yarns woven with natural weft yarns in a regular twill weave.

Desizing
An amylase enzyme rinse (desize) used to soften denim. A type of size such as cornstarch is added to the warp yarns prior to weaving in a process called slashing, which adds stiffness to the yarns. During the desizing step, the amylase enzyme attacks the starch and removes it from the fabric. Although this process reduces color slightly, it is primarily used to give a softness and drapability to denim.

Dips
Used to describe fabric or yarn when they are immersed in dye. Indigo yarns are usually dipped in an indigo bath six times.

GLOSSARY CONT.

Dual Ring-Spun
Also called "ring X ring." Signifies a denim weave in which both the warp and weft threads are made of ring-spun yarn. Creates a much softer and textured hand than both open-end and regular (single) ring-spun denim. Due to the additional labor required to produce dual ring-spun denim, it is usually only used by higher end, premium denim labels.

End
An individual warp yarn. Denim weaves are expressed as the number of ends per inch X the number of picks per inch. A typical denim weave is 66 X 46.

Enzymes
Enzymes, which are proteins present in all living cells, speed up chemical processes that would run very slowly if at all. They are non-toxic and readily broken down. Enzymes are used in textile processing, mainly in the finishing of fabrics and garments.

Enzyme Wash
Considered a more efficient and environmentally sound way to stone wash jeans. Rather than using pumice stones, organic enzymes (proteins) are used that eat away at the indigo. Jeans finished using enzymes tend to be stronger than those broken down by traditional stone washing, as the fabric is not subjected to the same level of abuse.

Filling Yarn
Also called weft yarn. Are the yarns that run crosswise, from selvage to selvage, in a weave.

Finishing
The techniques or processes performed on a garment, which give it its unique look. The Denim Design Lab is your own personal finishing laboratory.

GLOSSARY CONT.

Five Pocket Jeans
One of the most common styles of jeans; they have two back pockets, two front pockets and a coin pocket inside the right front pocket.

Garment Dye
A dyeing process preformed on finished garments, as opposed to a yarn dye, which takes place prior to the weaving of yarn. If you see pocket linings or labels that look the same color as the self-fabric, the garment was likely garment dyed.

Hand
A description of the way a fabric feels. A subjective judgment of the feel or hand of a fabric used to help decide if a fabric is suitable for a specific end use. The hand can be described as crisp, soft, drapable, smooth, springy, stiff, cool, warm, rough, hard, limp, soapy, etc. Finishing and garment wash will affect the final hand of a fabric.

Indigo
Blue vat dye that was originally derived from the "Indigofera tinctoria" plant by fermenting the leaves of the shrub. In 1987, 14 years after Adolf von Bayer identified the chemical structure of indigo, the chemical became synthetically manufactured. Indigo's inherent features are good colorfastness to water and light, a continual fading and its inability to penetrate fibers completely. This allows the blue color in jeans made dyed with indigo to always look irregular and individual. The majority of indigo used today is synthetically made. Natural indigo has a slightly red cast to it.

Iro-ochi
Japanese term referring to the fading of indigo dye in denim. The term specifically relates to fading in exposed areas and not across the entire garment. Your Denim Design Lab is designed to help you create "iro-ochi."

GLOSSARY CONT.

Jean
The term is possibly derived from the French word "genes." The term was originally used to describe the type of pants worn by sailors from Genoa. While the historical definition implied that all jeans were made of denim, the term jeans today can sometimes refer to a garment that has five pockets and be made from fabrics such as corduroy, twill or bull denim.

Laundry
In the "Denim Industry," a Laundry is a manufacturing company that takes unwashed jeans and processes them. This processing includes washing, stone washing, sandblasting, garment dyeing, and finishing. Laundries today are critical in making jeans look commercial and wash development has become as important as fabric development in the denim industry. The best laundries and wash developments come from the U.S., Japan and Italy. The "Denim Design Lab" is designed to help you recreate some of the vintage magic on individual pairs of denim, while the large laundries are able to reproduce denim treatments on a large scale.

Left-Hand Twill
Also know as an "S Twill." A weave in which the grain lines run from the top left-hand corner of the fabric towards the bottom right. Usually in piece-dyed fabrics, left-hand twill fabrics are woven from single plied yarns in the warp. The denim brand Lee has always used left-hand twill denim as its basic denim. Left-hand twills will often have a softer hand feel to them after washing then right-hand twills.

Loop Dyed
One of the three major industrial methods of dyeing indigo yarns.

Mercerization
An industrial process used on yarn or fabrics to increase its luster and dye affinity. For fabrics used in the denim

industry, mercerization can be used for keeping dye on the surface of the yarns or fabrics and to prevent dyes from fully penetrating the fibers.

Microsanding
In this fabric treatment process, a series of cylindrical rolls in a horizontal arrangement, either wrapped with an abrasive paper or chemically coated with an abrasive, are used to create a soft, sueded hand. The denim is pulled over the face of the sand rollers creating a raised surface finishing. Some color reduction is experienced.

Open-End Spinning
A spinning process in which individual fibers are fed into a high-speed rotor shaped like a cup where they begin to accumulate. Because not all of the fibers end up parallel to the axis of the yarn, the yarns produced using this method are not as strong as ring-spun yarns of the same size.

Overdye
A fabric dying process in which additional color is applied to the fabric or garment to create a different shade or cast. "Dirty Denim" is often created by applying a yellow overdye to denim. By localizing the application of the tint, you can create specific areas that look dirtier than the surrounding areas.

Oxidation
Occurs when oxygen and another substance chemically join and happens when indigo yarn comes out of the bath between dips.

Pick
A single weft yarn.

Pigment Dyes
Dyes that do not have an affinity for fiber and must therefore be held to the fabric with resins. They are available in almost

GLOSSARY CONT.

any color and are used extensively in the denim industry by fabric dyers who want to create fabrics that fade more easily.

Ply
All yarns are single ply unless twisted with another yarn. Plied yarns are used to make yarns stronger. In the denim industry, it has become important to ply yarns in piece dyed fabrics that are intended to endure a long stone wash cycle. The method of twisting and length of each yarn is a major determinant in the ultimate look and feel of the finished fabric.

Pumice Stones
Volcanic stone used for stone washing garments. Pumice is popular because of its strength and light weight. Before the use of pumice, rocks, plastic, shoes and just about every other material was used to wear down and soften denim during the laundry process.

Redline
See "Selvage."

Right-Hand Twill
Also know as a "Z Twill." The most common denim weave, in which the grain lines run from the top right-hand corner of the fabric towards the bottom left. Usually in piece-dyed fabrics right-hand twills use two plied yarns in the warp. Levi's has always used right-hand twills for its basic denim models.

Ring Dyeing
Describes a characteristic unique to indigo dye in which only the outer ring of the fibers in the yarn is dyed while the inner core remains white.

GLOSSARY cont.

Ring Spinning
A spinning process in which individual fibers are fed onto the end of the yarn while it is in the "twisting zone." The process consists of a ring, a ring traveler and a bobbin that rotates at high speed. The ring-spun yarn produced by this method creates unique surface characteristics in the fabric, including unevenness, which gives jeans an irregular authentic vintage look. Ring-spun yarns add strength, softness and character to denim fabric.

River Washing
A washing process using a combination of pumice stones and cellulose enzymes to give denim a vintage, worn hand. The washer is loaded only with stones and fabric for the first cycle. Enzymes are introduced for the second stage in combination with the stones and they are tumbled until a naturally aged look is produced.

Rivet
A metal accessory that is used for reinforcement of stress points as well as for nonfunctional ornamentation.

Rope Dying
Considered the best possible method to dye indigo yarns. The threads of denim yarn are twisted into a rope, which is then fed through a sequence of being dipped into a bath of indigo dye, followed by exposure to air, multiple times. The frequency determines the ultimate shade of blue.

Sanding / Emerising
A fabric finishing process where fabrics are sanded (with real sandpaper) to make the surface soft without hair. It can be performed before or after dying. Your Denim Design Lab contains various types of coated abrasives to help you finish your denim by hand sanding.

GLOSSARY CONT.

Sanforize
A pre-shrinking fabric process that limits residual fabric shrinkage to under 1%. Developed in the late 1920s by the Sanforize Co., the process was used in 1947 to treat garments in Wrangler's first jeans line. The process includes the stretching and manipulation of the denim cloth before it is washed. Raw, un-sanforized jeans will shrink 7-10% after the first wash, and continue to shrink slightly up to through the third wash.

Sandblasting
A laundry process performed before washing in which jeans are shot with guns of sand in order to abrade them and cause a worn appearance. While originally done by hand, this process is now automated at most large laundry houses.

Selvage
Also referred to as "Redline" or "Aka-Mimi." Originally called "self-edge." This is the narrow tightly woven band on either edge of the denim fabric, parallel to the warp. A selvage end prevents the edge of the denim from unraveling. Old 28 to 30 inch shuttle looms produce denim where selvages are closed, whereas on the larger modern weaving machines, the weft yarn is cut on every pick, creating what is called a "fringe" selvage. Colored thread was used by Cone Mills to identify the particular fabric used by its major manufacturers. Vintage Levi's jeans began with an all white strip and later had a single red strip along both selvages, Lee's had a blue or green strip along one end and Wrangler's was yellow. Each Denim Design Lab is constructed using 100% red selvage denim from Cone Denim, which helps us to accurately recreate various vintage washes on each kit.

Shade Batching
The process of selecting batches of fabrics into homogeneous shade lots to obtain consistent color continuity in garment making.

GLOSSARY cont.

Shade Blanket
Fabric is cut from each roll of fabric and sewn together with roll numbers on the back of each pad to allow manufacturers to wash and identify all shade colors of each roll. This is an important tool in cutting apparel made from denim to ensure that garments from the same shade group are cut.

Shed
During the weaving process, this is the opening formed by raising and lowering the warp yarns on a loom. The shed opening is what the weft yarns are passed through to complete the weaving interlace.

Shuttle
The device that carries the weft yarn across the loom in vintage shuttle looms. Selvage denim can only be woven using a shuttle loom.

Silhouette
Refers to the shape of a garment (i.e. bootleg, relaxed, low-rise, slim, carpenter, etc.).

Sizing
Starch, gelatin glue or wax that is added to fabrics in the finishing stage to improve touch or weight and to help fabric laying in the cutting phase. Denim fabrics, for example can have almost one ounce of sizing.

Skewing
Refers to the occurrence of twisting that happens when the fabric shrinks more perpendicular to the twill line than along the twill line. Without compensating for this occurrence, the twill line will cause the right angles that the fabric is woven in to torque approximately five degrees after washing. To compensate for this, denim is skewed about five degrees in the same direction as the twill line to prevent the side seam from twisting to the front of the jean. You will often find authentic vintage jeans with one or both of the side seams twisted towards the front of the jean... now you know why.

GLOSSARY CONT.

Slasher Dyeing
One of the three main methods of dyeing indigo yarn.

Sliver
In the yarn manufacturing process, a sliver refers to the loose, soft, untwisted rope of cotton fibers that is produced using the carding machine.

Slub
Refers to thick or heavy places in the yarn. Slubs and other inconsistencies are common in denim produced on vintage shuttle looms. Modern yarn spinning technology is able to engineer these vintage looking textures into yarn in a pre-defined manner.

Stone Washing
A process that physically removes color and adds contrast. A 20-yard roll of fabric, generally 62 inches in width, is put into a 250-pound washing machine along with pumice stones. The fabric and stones are rotated together for a set period of time. The washing time dictates the final color of the fabric - the longer the denim and stones are rotated the lighter the color becomes and more contrast is achieved. The denim is then rinsed, softened and tumble dried. Both Marithé & François Girbau from France and the Japanese jeans giant "Edwin" claim to have pioneered this finishing technique.

Tate-ochi
Japanese term referring to occurrences of "Iro-ochi" forming in vertical lines in vintage denim. As the thread width is not uniform in vintage denim, the color fades the most where the thread is the thickest. This creates a white or severely faded thread of several centimeters along a single vertical indigo thread.

Twill
The diagonal lines formed by the weave.

GLOSSARY CONT.

Warp
The lengthwise vertical yarns woven into the weft yarns. They usually have more twist and are stronger than weft yarns.

Weave
The combination of warp and weft yarns to produce different weave designs. The warp face designs used in denim are called out by the number of weft yarns that the warp ends pass over, followed by the number of weft yarns they pass under. Some of the most common denim weaves are 3x1, 2x1 and 3x1 broken twill. The 3x1 and 2x1 can be made in left or right-hand twill directions. 3x1 right-hand twill is the most common denim design.

Weft
The un-dyed, crosswise filling yarns used in denim weave.

Whiskering
A fading of the ridges in creases in the crotch area and back of the knees, which gives the appearance of aged denim; can also be the inverse - dark creased in faded denim. Your Denim Design Lab is designed to help you create authentic looking whiskers.

XX
The name used to originally reference a particular model of Levi's jeans built prior to 1890. The XX has been present ever since, and is used as both a lot or ordering number and to signify Levi's highest quality denim, "501 XX," woven by Cone Denim.

Yarn Dye
Refers to fabric in which the individual yarns are dyed prior to weaving. Denim is a yarn dyed fabric.

ACKNOWLEDGMENTS

Special thanks to Lynn Downey of LS&CO., Jennifer Johnson of Lee Jeans and the crew at Cone Denim for fact-checking numerous versions of the manuscript and providing such amazing photographs. Equal thanks and appreciation to Tom McKenna, Kara Nicholas, Mary Black, Josephine Palermo and Phil Goetz from Cone Denim for their continued support and guidance throughout the DDL™ project. Thanks to "Curb" and Takumi for being great sounding boards, and to Troung for going the extra mile with the kits. Thanks to Jeff Park and Christian Troy for their help with the editing of the manuscript.

Most of all… thanks to my wife Delia for keeping our lives moving during the painfully slow creation of Denim Design Lab, "I Love You!!"

Photo Credits

All photographs © 2005 Brian Robbins, except as noted under the particular image and/or as follows:

1, 2, 3, 4, 5: Courtesy of LS&CO. Archives; 6: Courtesy of Carhartt; 7 (top): Courtesy of LS&CO. Archives; 7 (bottom), 8, 9: Courtesy of Lee Jeans Archives; 10: Library of Congress, Prints & Photographs Division, FSA-OWI Collection, LC-USF34-034084-D, photograph by Russell Lee; 11: Courtesy of LS&CO. Archives; 12, 13: Courtesy of Lee Jeans Archives; 14: Courtesy of LS&CO. Archives; 15: © John Springer Collection/CORBIS; 16: © Bettmann/CORBIS; 17, 18, 19: Courtesy of Lee Jeans Archives; 20: Courtesy of LS&CO. Archives; 22: © Bettmann/CORBIS; 24, 28, 29: Courtesy of Lee Jeans Archives; 31: Library of Congress, Prints & Photographs Division, LC-USZ62-116585 & LC-USZ62-116586; 33: Library of Congress, Prints & Photographs Division, LC-USZC2-3753; 35: Library of Congress, Prints & Photographs Division, LC-USZ62-53584; 36, 37: Courtesy of Lee Jeans Archives; 43: Courtesy of LS&CO. Archives; 46, 47, 48, 49, 50: Courtesy of Lee Jeans Archives; 51, 52, 53, 54: Courtesy of Lee Jeans Archives; 56: Library of Congress, Prints & Photographs Division, FSA-OWI Collection, LC-USF34-046284-D; 57: Library of Congress, Prints & Photographs Division, FSA-OWI Collection, LC-USF34-031966-D; 59, 61, 62: Cone Denim Archival Collection; 64,

ACKNOWLEDGMENTS

65, 66, 67: Courtesy of LS&CO. Archives, photographs by Hangauer/Kissinger; 68, 69, 72: Courtesy of LS&CO. Archives; 70, 71, 73, 78, 79, 80: Courtesy of Lee Jeans Archives; 74, 75, 76, 77: Cone Denim Archival Collection, photographs by Christopher Clancy; 126-138: Courtesy of LS&CO. Archives.

Sources

Cone Denim, "Half Century Book 1891-1941"
Cone Denim, "Cone - A Century of Excellence 1891-1991"
Cone Denim, "Found"
Cone Denim, "The Denim Manufacturing Process"
David Little, "Vintage Denim," 1996
Lee, "American History: Lee Jeans 101"
LS&CO., "This is a Pair of Levi's Jeans... The Official History of the Levi's Brand," 1995
LS&CO., "Levi Strauss: A Short Biography"
Lynn Downey, "A Short History of Denim"
Lynn Downey, "The Invention of Levi's® 501® Jeans"

DEDICATION

Diego Robbins
Sporting his first pair of DDL™ "Jr. Mechanics"

NOTES

NOTES

NOTES